THE VITAL
SINGLES MINISTRY

EFFECTIVE
CHURCH
SERIES

HARRY ODUM

Edited by HERB MILLER

THE VITAL
SINGLES MINISTRY

ABINGDON PRESS

Nashville

THE VITAL SINGLES MINISTRY

Copyright © 1992 by Harry Odum

This book is printed on recycled, acid-free paper.

Library of Congress Cataloging-in-Publication Data

Odum, Harry, 1940—
    The vital sinlges ministry / Harry Odum; edited by Herb Miller.
        p.   cm. — (Effective church series)
    Includes bibliographical references.
    ISBN 0-687-43800-4 (alk. paper)
    1. Church work with single people. I. Miller, Herb. II. Title. III. Series.

BV639.S5028   1991
259'.08'652—dc20   91-42511
                                                                      CIP

Scripture quotations are from the New Revised Standard Version of the
Bible, copyright 1989 by the Division of Christian Education of the National
Council of the Churches of Christ in the USA. Used by permission.

MANUFACTURED IN THE UNITED STATES OF AMERICA

This book is dedicated to the hundreds of lay people who gave of their time and energy to develop the Phoenix class. Without their tireless and creative efforts, Phoenix would not exist. To the past officers for their leadership; to the teachers for their dedication; to those who gave of their time to work in the workshops, retreats, social activities, and fund-raisers; and to those who pitched in when a little extra help was needed and made the difference.

ACKNOWLEDGMENTS

To Herb Miller, to whom I cannot offer enough thanks for his help with the editing of this book. Without his assistance, this book would never have made it to press. Also, to Sarah Harvey, who edited the book enough to get it accepted by Abingdon Press. Also, to Patti Jones and Marian Burris for their assistance in double checking the editor's recommendations. Finally, to Christ Methodist Church and the Phoenix class for leading the way into the future of singles ministries, both led by Dr. Bob Pierson, a man of vision.

CONTENTS

FOREWORD

After glancing at a job applicant's paperwork, a personnel department interviewer said, "I see that you've been careful not to become overqualified."

Most congregations fit into that category when they think of organizing a ministry for the thousands of divorced, never-married, and widowed singles in their community. Yes, most church leaders believe the Church is for everyone. They have the desire to involve and serve singles, and they instinctively know that the pastoral care they are giving these persons is not enough. Singles need a caring group, not just a caring pastor. Yet, most of these pastors and lay leaders feel under-qualified to accomplish this important leadership role.

Harry Odum meets this need by providing the how-to-do-it tools for this specialized field. Following his instructions will help to protect visionary dreams from becoming a nightmare of well-intentioned failures. The five reasons why congregations should establish a singles ministry make an excellent platform for communicating this need to church leaders: (1) because the 1950s birthed a new culture that contains a sea of singles; (2) because many of these singles are walking wounded in need of emotional and spiritual repair from traumatic experiences; (3) because singles ministries sponsored by churches can help heal these hurts; (4) because most singles do not feel comfortable in other church classes or groups; and (5) because singles ministries can strengthen a church's overall ministry effectiveness. Building on these five foundational presuppositions, Odum provides detailed prescriptions for starting, growing, and maintaining an effective singles ministry in churches of every size.

Justice Oliver Wendell Holmes is reported to have said that he would not give a fig for the simplicity on *this side* of complexity but that he would give his life for the simplicity on *the other side* of complexity. Odum helps us make that trip regarding singles ministries. He moves us through the maze of over-simplified anecdotes offered by countless amateur advisers to the simplicity that lies beyond complexity.

Odum's leadership insights fit the goal of the Effective Church Series: to help meet the need for "how to" answers in specific areas of church life. Each of these volumes provides clergy and laypersons with practical insights and methods that can increase their congregation's effectiveness in achieving God's purposes in every aspect of ministry: leadership, worship, Sunday school, membership care, biblical literacy, spiritual growth, small groups, evangelism, new-member assimilation, prayer, youth work, singles work, young adult work, time management, stewardship, administration, community service, world mission, conflict resolution, and writing skills.

Odum's insights also fit the theological focus of the Effective Church Series. While concentrating more on the practical "how-to-do-it" than on the theoretical and conceptual, its "ideas that work" rest on biblical principles. Without that foundation, method sharing feeds us a diet of cotton candy, sweet but devoid of nutrients. Odum has addressed the subject of singles ministries in ways consistent with biblical truths and classic Christian theology.

A woman driving through the mountains in a blinding snowstorm became frightened. She could not see more than a dozen feet ahead. How relieved she was to see the tailgate of a snowplow in front of her. As the truck crept forward, she followed it. "This is certainly slow, but it is very safe," she thought.

After a few miles, the truck stopped. The driver got out

and walked back to her car. "Where are you going?" he asked. After she described her destination, he said, "I appreciate the company, but you are not likely to get there by following me. This parking lot that I am plowing out does not lead in that direction."

Odum's observations are general enough to help every kind of singles group—but specific enough to keep groups out of the parking lots, ditches, and canyons that are so common to this ministry.

INTRODUCTION

Nothing in the world is single,
All things by law divine
In spirit meet and mingle.
—*Percy B. Shelley,* Love's Philosophy *(1819)*

Starting a singles group in their church? The idea sounded great to the five people who met at a restaurant to discuss it. They launched the plan with enthusiasm. But nine months later their singles group had evaporated—their idea consigned to the scrap pile of dead dreams that had sounded good but failed to fly.

That story reruns in several thousand churches each year. Even though initiated by sincere, committed people, the majority of singles ministries crash and burn. A postmortem on the wreckage usually indicates that one or more malfunctions caused the crash: (1) the singles ministry did not have a focused direction; (2) the leaders did not know what types of content to use in the classes or groups; or (3) the leaders did not know how to organize the ministry. The purpose of this book is to help your church form a successful singles ministry by avoiding these three major malfunctions and countless smaller ones. If your church already has a singles ministry, use the book as a resource to strengthen its long-term health.

The principles, methods, and ideas outlined here apply to

churches of every size. Whether you have ten singles in a small-town church in North Dakota or a thousand singles in a New York City congregation, you will find insights that apply to your situation. So avoid the assumption that a small church cannot develop an effective singles ministry. Group size does not determine success or failure in this endeavor. Small ministries with less than a dozen members can have a caring, successful program. Large churches with a hundred or more singles in their programs can fail. Jesus said, "For where two or three are gathered in my name, I am there among them" (Matthew 18:20). Nowhere will people more powerfully experience that truth than in a small singles group. Do not let the size of your church discourage you. A handful of singles can develop an effective ministry.

This book is reality-based, not theory-based. The ideas come from two major sources: (1) singles ministries in churches of various denominations throughout the United States, and (2) the experiences of the Phoenix Class at Christ United Methodist Church, Tulsa, Oklahoma. Thus we will approach this subject from both a general and a specific viewpoint. We will use both binoculars that scan the horizon and a microscope that analyzes one incredibly successful singles ministry. The Phoenix Class is an excellent parable platform, because it illustrates many of the principles and methods essential to forming and maintaining an effective singles ministry. These ideas enabled the Phoenix Class to become one of the largest Sunday school "classes" in America, married or single (most churches have a total membership smaller than that of the Phoenix Class).

Phoenix is a perfect symbol for the central purpose of a singles program. According to an ancient Arabian legend, the Phoenix bird, consumed by fire, arose out of its ashes every five hundred years to begin anew, more beautiful than before. People who divorce can rise out of the ashes of their fallen marriages with lives more beautiful and fulfilling than before. While that mission is not the only reason for a singles ministry, it is one of the most important reasons. If a singles group succeeds at that ministry, it will likely succeed in its ministry to other types of singles.

INTRODUCTION

Although churches do not establish a singles ministry in order to enlarge their memberships, the Phoenix symbol can apply to congregations, also. During 1982, for example, the average United Methodist congregation declined in membership. But Christ United Methodist Church in Tulsa enjoyed a 24 percent net increase in membership that year. The Phoenix Class began 1982 with 375 members and ended the year with 950 members, which enabled Christ Church to experience healthy growth.

Tom King, a man recently divorced, wanted to start a Sunday school class especially for single adults. He approached the senior pastor with the idea. Dr. Pierson, previously divorced himself, agreed. Tom assembled a group of eight single people, and on the first Sunday in April 1974, Phoenix began. Starting a singles ministry was a bold step in those days, because most churches did not look upon singles favorably. The class developed slowly, but as more singles heard about Phoenix, it grew at a steady rate. The leaders structured the class, elected officers, and added leadership positions as the need arose. Phoenix gradually became known throughout the Tulsa area as "that Singles Group at Christ Methodist." Singles who needed a church home attended Sunday school, and many of them joined the church as a direct result of attending Phoenix.

By 1980, Phoenix had grown to about 200 members. (Phoenix now has 1,100 active members, larger than most small towns in Oklahoma and larger than 90 percent of the 350,000 churches in the United States.) This did not happen overnight. The program developed and improved over a ten-year period, through much trial and error by far-sighted and hard-working leaders. The senior pastor, Dr. Bob Pierson, totally supported Phoenix in its early years, and still does—a primary reason for its spectacular growth. He envisioned Phoenix as a large class from the Sunday it formed. He gave it a place to happen, and he let the leaders develop it in their own way. Time has proven Dr. Pierson a prophet concerning singles ministries and their place in American church life.

Not all of the methods and ideas in this book will fit

without modification in congregations of every denomination. Different churches have different traditions and rules. Some permit dancing, some do not. Some insist on separate classes for men and women, some do not. Thus you may find it necessary to modify these procedures as you tailor-make a singles program consistent with your church's beliefs and doctrines. These general guidelines have, however, worked in churches of many denominations, and they will work in yours.

I

WHY A SINGLES MINISTRY?

And the LORD God said, "It is not good that the man should be alone; I will make him a helper as his partner." —Genesis 2:18

"I can't see why they don't come to our class. We would love to have them."

"Looks to me like a bunch of people who aren't really serious about church. We're in the religious business here, not in the entertainment business. I vote against it."

"There aren't that many of those kind of people in our town. Why bother?"

"Better put our energy into youth work. That's the future of the church."

One or more of these four reservations usually appear anytime church leaders discuss this subject. So, the first step in forming or strengthening a singles ministry involves dealing with these honest concerns. Why does our church need a special ministry for singles? Why not let singles and married people go to the same class? What makes these people so different? Like everything else our church undertakes, we must define clear answers to the questions about "why" we should embark on a ministry. Otherwise, we will lack the motivation to look for and hear answers to the "how-to-do-it" questions.

Why a singles ministry? That question has at least five answers.

Because the 1950s Birthed a New Culture

The singles culture is a new phenomenon. Before the 1950s, family units were the backbone of church and society. Since then, our society has changed, especially the institution of marriage. We heard of few people divorcing before World War II. Now divorce is as commonplace as marriage. We have grown accustomed to new habits. We expect that one-half of the people who say yes at the altar will say no in the courtroom.

During World War II, a major change occurred in the life-style of Americans. Many wives started working outside the home. While their husbands fought in far-off foxholes, women took over the essential jobs of running our country. After the war, many women did not want to merely return to the traditional roles of being wife and mother. They enjoyed their place in the job market, because they found an identity they had never known before and a feeling of independence. Wives no longer depended on their husbands for survival.

During the transitional decade of the 1940s, the roles of men and women became confused. Since the dawn of time (we thought), men had expected to provide the food; women had expected to cook it and take care of the children. During the 1950s, male-female role confusion that began bubbling in the 1940s solidified into a new set of complications. In the 1960s, the divorce rate soared, and previously unthinkable family configurations forced shocked parents and grandparents to adjust to new life-style patterns.

The news of broken homes stormed through society and churches in much the same way AIDS did in the 1980s. America had given birth to a new culture, an unacceptable one—single adults. The wives and husbands who together fought for survival during the Depression and World War II believed in marriage until death separated them. They married "for better or worse, in sickness and in health, for richer or poorer." And they reared their children with the same traditional viewpoint concerning marriage. By the 1960s, that era appeared to be over.

Most churches have always taught against divorce, and rightfully so. Nothing devastates a person, family, or social mores as does the break up of a marriage. The Bible teaches us to stay married. "But I say to you that anyone who divorces his wife, except on the ground of unchastity, causes her to commit adultery; and whoever marries a divorced woman commits adultery" (Matthew 5:32).

Now, we had divorced people popping up everywhere. They went against their parents' basic moral teachings, society's mores, and the churches' classic moral authority. In this initial wave of change, divorced people found few sympathetic ears. The shame and guilt associated with their divorces intensified as society branded them as outcasts. Many "normal" parents discouraged their children from playing with youngsters from broken homes. Single mothers had difficulty finding places to rent. Employers did not want to hire divorced people. Churches did not know what to do with them. Single people were shunned.

We cannot blame the churches or society for this attitude. No one expected the divorce boom or knew what to do about it. "Shuffle them off into a corner," everyone seemed to think; "maybe they will go away." But they did not. Divorce—a cancer—spread rapidly, its tentacles penetrating into the lifestream of American society. Few families, and no economic class, religious affiliation, or job position escaped. The singles culture became the fastest growing section of the American population. Divorce even began sneaking into the ranks of ordained ministers. Talk about trauma! Ministers do not get divorced. They are role models for the rest of us. One church immediately stripped its divorced pastor of his duties. He had founded the church that later turned its back on him! The last time I heard from him, he worked in a gas station.

Before the 1950s, widowed and never-married people had made up most of the singles culture. Suddenly, multitudes of divorced people joined their ranks. This new group of

21

singles, however, had quite different feelings, attitudes, and problems than widows and never-marrieds. Widowed persons may feel anger at a disease, a car accident, or another unexpected cause of death, but they do not have a living ex-spouse toward whom they feel anger. Widowed persons still must deal with the trauma of living single in a marriage-oriented world, but they do not have to worry about running into their former mates at the grocery store or in church. They do not have to fuss over custody of the children or bother themselves about child-support payments or alimony.

The never-marrieds do not have the same challenges to deal with as this mass of divorced persons. The never-marrieds do not have to deal with anger at an ex-spouse or anger at a death. They usually do not have children to raise alone. Yet, they do have to deal with questions such as "Why haven't you ever married? Is something wrong with you, and no one wants you? Are you gay? Are you a selfish person who doesn't want to share your life with someone else?" Society looked down on never-marrieds because they did not follow the traditional, expected activities of society—marrying and having a mortgage, two kids, and a station wagon. Yet, their social stigma was far less than that of divorced persons.

The churches of the 1960s knew they needed to change to meet the needs of the ever-growing singles population, but what were they to do? Most singles felt uncomfortable in married Sunday school classes. They were different, or at least everyone thought so. And in some ways, they did feel and act different. Many persons, after a divorce, quit going to church. In some cases, both partners feel that they have sinned against God and society. The shame and guilt caused by the divorce can create burdens that feel as heavy as an anvil.

Divorced singles have the same spiritual and emotional needs as married people. When they feel separated from their church home, where do they go to get these needs met? Churches have a reputation for stepping in to help when a death occurs in the family, a member goes to the hospital, or any of the other calamities can hit us. But churches did not know what to do with the multiplying numbers of reminted singles.

At first, many churches did not give the singles a whole-hearted welcome in their services. Times have changed. As divorce ate its way deeper into the population, more religious institutions wanted to start special programs for the singles. But what kind? How? Where? When? Churches tried to meet the needs of singles, but found it difficult. Thousands of singles ministries started but lasted only a short while. Ordained ministers, most of them married, sympathized more as the years passed. However, they did not know what to do to help, because they did not understand—*really* understand from experience. How many preachers had lived the life of a single? How many had known the heartbreak of a broken home? Seminaries did not include courses on how to deal with massive numbers of divorced people.

Because Singles Hurt

People who have never been divorced or widowed do not realize the trauma you experience when your marriage partner asks for a divorce, or someone tells you that your mate is dead. The writer of Psalms said it perfectly:

My heart is in anguish within me,
    the terrors of death have fallen upon me.
Fear and trembling come upon me,
    and horror overwhelms me.
And I say, "O that I had wings like a dove!
    I would fly away and be at rest;
truly, I would flee far away;
    I would lodge in the wilderness." (Psalm 55:4-7)

Every segment of your life changes. Troubles charge over the horizon like a herd of mad bulls, threatening survival. Unanswered questions flow at you from all directions: "What do I do with the incredible loneliness I feel? I feel like a loser;

am I? How do I rebuild my life? How can I trust another person with my feelings? What do I do about my limited finances? I'm a sexual being; now what? My children are experiencing their own turmoil; how do I help them? I need to laugh again; where can I find some fun in my life to lighten this soul-smothering pain I'm feeling? How do I get the anger, hate, and bitterness out of my system? Where can I find peace again?"

The collapse of a marriage can be life threatening. In *Singles, the New Americans* Jacqueline Simenauer and David Carroll reveal that 34 percent of the men polled and 45 percent of the women reported increased depression during the first year of being single. Seventeen percent of the men *occasionally* considered suicide, as did 29 percent of the women. Two percent of the men and 3 percent of the women *often* considered suicide. Two percent of the men and 4 percent of the women *attempted* suicide. In other words, *one out of four* newly single persons at least consider taking their lives during that first painful year.

When a marriage or a spouse dies, the survivors face a wilderness as desolate as the followers of Moses who faced the barrenness of the unknown desert. What lay ahead? Which direction should they take? They did not know. When they found themselves trapped by the Red Sea and the bad guys racing after them, they felt betrayed by God and feared for their lives. Where to go? They could not go backward or forward.

> He sustained him in a desert land,
>   in a howling wilderness waste;
> he shielded him, cared for him,
>   guarded him as the apple of his eye.
> As an eagle stirs up its nest,
>   and hovers over its young;
> as it spreads its wings, takes them up,
>   and bears them aloft on its pinions,
> the Lord alone guided him;
>   no foreign god was with him.
>   —Deuteronomy 32:10-12

Newly divorced and widowed persons feel the same frustration and fear. They must wander alone in the wilderness of society. They do not know in which direction to turn for guidance. They face a bleak, uncertain future, blocked by an ocean of problems. They have come to a new place in life, and one to which they probably did not want to arrive. Moses' followers had one another. Most newly singled people must strike out alone, not knowing what the future holds for them. The past haunts them, and they struggle to live without pain in the present, as they try to build themselves a future. Unanswered questions and problems create giant gaps in their lives that they cannot fill by themselves.

Most singles must face the formidable major problem of human sexuality. Many ask themselves, "What to do now that I'm single?" "I've remained faithful to one person for these many years," some say. "What do I do about sex; do I or don't I? Must I? I can't . . . but I have desires." The Bible teaches about sex outside marriage, and about adultery. Where can the singles turn for help? After all, most churches preach against extramarital sex and divorce.

What about the innocent bystanders, the children? Youngsters in divorced families lack the daily support and guidance of both parents. Their home has changed forever. Their security is threatened. How difficult a time will the single parent alone have raising the children? What feelings do youngsters experience when they cannot see one of their parents every day? Do both sets of grandparents get to see their grandchildren again? What emotional impact does a remarriage have on the children?

Singles and their families need help. They are alone, scared, depressed, worried, and changing from the married culture to the singles culture. Where do they turn? If not to a church, where else? Did not Jesus do his miracles among those who hurt the most? Why should not his continuing body—the church—organize to let singles ministries perform the miracles that no one else can do as well as they can?

What happens to a family during a divorce? What is so

traumatic about it? Why does a broken family find it so difficult to fit back into society?

Let's take a look at a hypothetical couple, Jack and Jill. They have two kids, Billy and Sally. They live in a house with a white picket fence, own a station wagon and a bouncing, yapping white poodle dog, Skippy. Jack and Jill have fulfilled the Great American Dream.

One morning, Jack—after fifteen years of marriage—realizes he and Jill have more serious marriage problems than they can solve. Marriage counseling has not helped. The marriage has ended for all practical purposes.

"What will we do?" Jack asks Jill, voice breaking with the pain of knowing divorce lies in their future. Divorce. Surely not. That happens to other families.

"I don't know," Jill responds, wiping the tears from her cheeks, thoughts turning to Billy and Sally. How to tell them? Do they already suspect?

Jack and Jill sadly gaze into each other's eyes. Each sees not the person they promised, as young adults in love, to cherish until death. Not the person with whom they shared the joyful births of Billy and Sally. Not the person with whom they struggled beside to build their Great American Dream. They each now see a stranger, a person they no longer know, a person with whom they can no longer communicate, a person they no longer love. Strangers in the day, and in the night.

Painful words that neither needs to vocalize come to their minds. "We've worked together to provide a Christian home for Billy and Sally, to send them to the best schools, and to love them." Jack stares down at his clenched fists, knuckles white from the pressure and sadness he feels. I've failed, he thinks. Our home is breaking apart. He thinks of living alone without Jill and the children.

Jill breaks down, her mind overwhelmed by the image of her and the children living alone in a small apartment, without Jack. I've failed, she thinks. We married for better or worse, in sickness or in health, in riches or poor, but. . . .

"Must our marriage end?" Jack asks, remembering the love he and Jill felt for each other in years past—the struggles, the triumphs, and the joy they felt at the births of Billy and Sally.

"I don't know what else to do," Jill responds. The memories of shattered dreams flow through her mind. "We've tried everything, marriage counseling, talking, and even going off together."

She chokes back the tears. "Jack . . . it's over."

Knowing she is right, Jack walks into the living room and stares out the picture window, watching Billy and Sally playing kickball with their friends.

Jill, filled with pain and anger, goes to the kitchen to prepare lunch, the wound so stinging that she feels as if her soul is on fire. This isn't happening to our family, she thinks, banging a pan on the top of the new range she and Jack bought just last week.

Billy and Sally open the front door and race toward the kitchen to see what Mom's fixing for lunch. Seeing their daddy standing by the picture window, tears running down his cheeks, stops them. Fear fills their young minds. They look at each other, and the silent thought hits them both. Divorce. Billy and Sally have known for several months that serious problems existed between Daddy and Mom. Children, more often than not, know about coming catastrophes.

Jack turns from the window. "Kids, Mom and I have something to tell you."

Hearing the exchange, Jill steps into the living room and sits on the couch, her eyes reddened and puffy from crying.

"You're getting a divorce," Billy stammers, eyes filling with tears and lower lip trembling uncontrollably.

"Please don't," Sally pleads, heart pounding with naked fear. "What about our family? Where will we live? Who will we live with?" Her young mind valiantly struggles to deal with the looming death of her family unit.

Jack and Jill look at each other. Neither can speak. A black cloud of sadness settles over the once-loving family.

Billy and Sally sit on the floor, holding hands, trying to gain strength from each other, both sobbing so hard they can barely breathe. They have seen the pain and devastation many of their friends experienced when their parents divorced.

"We've tried to make our marriage work," Jill says. "But, . . . " she takes a deep breath, "I'm sorry."

Lunch forgotten, the four go to separate rooms in a vain attempt to deal with their emotions. They are not successful. Too much pain.

News of the divorce rapidly spreads through the P.T.A. and the church. "Have you heard that Jack and Jill are divorcing? What will happen to little Billy and Sally?" friends whisper among themselves.

Other couples, now self-conscious when around either Jack or Jill and not knowing what to do or say to comfort the family, stay away and stop calling. For the first time in their lives, Jack and Jill feel too ashamed and embarrassed to go to church. So they quit attending, losing contact with their friends and church. They also lose the spiritual support of that association when they need it the most.　　　·

Jack and Jill file the divorce papers, and the legal separation begins. Jill and the children continue to live in the family home. Jack moves to a small efficiency apartment on the other side of town. To their dismay, the money does not stretch far enough to keep both homes going. The legal fees were not in their budget, and the extra rent and utilities Jack incurs add to the burden. Two families cannot live as cheaply as one.

Family members take sides, some on Jack's and some on Jill's. His family points their fingers at Jill for the divorce and hers blames Jack. The innocent victims, Billy and Sally, feel torn between the parents. Each wonders if they did something to cause the divorce and if they have done anything to prevent it? They feel guilt and shame the same as their parents.

One night, Jack goes to get the children, taking them to eat pizza and to a movie. The three feel the tension of something missing—Jill. Their family unit has changed.

Time passes and the divorce becomes final. All those concerned find themselves broken, financially and emotionally. The Great American Dream dies hard and takes no prisoners.

Now single adults, Jack's and Jill's lives change forever.

Jack sees Billy and Sally every other weekend, and their relationship improves as time passes.

Now Jack finds his life one of solitude and loneliness. Child support and alimony drain his funds, leaving him little money to date, even if he wanted to, but he does not. He goes to work, comes home, watches television, and goes to bed. He repeats the schedule every day, except every other weekend when Billy and Sally stay with him.

Billy and Sally also feel the frustration, fear, anger, and loneliness that accompany divorce. Billy's grades plummet. He causes problems during class, loses interest in sports, and withdraws into himself. Sally does not go out to play with her friends anymore and has problems sleeping at night. She fights with Jill over the smallest detail. Fear of the future dominates the children's thoughts. Where will they live? Will they have enough money to live? Will their dad and mom marry someone else, and turn their love toward their new mate? Will Jack see them anymore? Both Billy and Sally decide they will never marry. Marriage causes pain.

Although she has custody of the children, Jill longs for adult company. She occasionally meets a man and dates some. But Billy and Sally refuse to accept them, treating them discourteously. Jill finds it hard to maintain new relationships.

Each night is a rerun of those before it. Exhausted after a long hard day at work (she had never worked outside the home while married), she still must do the cooking, ironing, and cleaning before depositing her saddened, tired body into bed for another fitful night's sleep. Billy needs new basketball shoes and Sally a new coat, but she cannot afford them. Jack helps as much as he can, but it is not enough. "I wonder what crisis tomorrow will bring?" she mumbles just before drifting off into the troubled never-never land of the depressed. Her life is inhibited by fears of the unpaid utility bills. Will she have enough money to give Billy and Sally lunch money for the coming week?

Meanwhile, lonesome Jack starts to live the single delusions of the American male. After getting a raise in pay, he buys new clothes and rents a bigger apartment. With cat-like grace, he dives head-long into the bubbling, swinging night life of the "world of singles."

Never had he realized so many single women existed. Everywhere he goes, they make themselves available. Jack, acting like a cool, suave bachelor, hardly knows where to begin. The menu of the "world of singles" has blondes, redheads, and brunettes. He decides he will try the entire menu before death parts him from ecstasy. Jack rockets into the sparkling depths of the night life of the American single. A few months pass. Then, one morning—after a long night —he realizes he has created an emotionally shallow world for himself. He has grown tired of the nightly party arena.

At first, he does not understand what is wrong with his life. Then, in a tearful moment, he admits he is lonesome and misses life as a parent and husband. No longer can he kiss Billy and Sally each morning on their way to school. The nights seem long and lonely. The blondes, redheads, and brunettes merge into one rainbow of endless and unfulfilling involvements. He finds no pot of gold.

The next day he calls some of his married friends. To his dismay, he realizes they no longer have anything in common. He discovers that some couples he and Jill knew have taken her side and have little to say to him. With a deep sadness, Jack now knows that his part of the Great American Dream has crashed. His life-style is different from the one he lived for fifteen years. The time has come for him to accept his new place in life. He is now a part of a culture with a different set of rules and customs than the one he had as a married person.

Jack now knows he needs to find people with whom he can feel comfortable. "Church," he thinks. "I have not been to church for months. But, my old one? . . . nah, out of the question," he decides. What if someone he knows should ask him what happened to his marriage? What if he should see Jill with a male friend? Could he handle the trauma of seeing Billy and Sally going to his church with another man? Jack decides against going to church.

Jack needs people he can relate to, people who understand

his place in life. He needs to be around someone who comprehends the life of a single father living without his children.

"Jill's lucky," he tells a co-worker. "She lives with Billy and Sally in our old house. Her life hasn't changed as much as mine."

Unknown to Jack, Jill stays home from church for the same reasons. She knows the kids miss their Sunday school friends, and she misses the worship services. What to do? Her church does not have a class for single adults. Jill feels uncomfortable when she thinks of attending a class with married couples in it.

"Jack's probably having the time of his life," she says to a friend one cold, rainy night. "He can go and come as he pleases. If he gets lonesome, he can get dressed and go find some women to date. I love my kids, but I would enjoy having male company occasionally."

She blows on the steaming cup of hot chocolate before taking a sip. "Women sure have a hard time in the single world," she says, gazing into the warm, crackling fireplace. "I need to find a support group of single people like myself. The nightclub scene won't satisfy my needs as an adult. Though I'm around people, it's a shallow way of life. I've met some friendly people, but we never become good friends. I enjoy visiting my married friends, but it's not enough. Our lives are now worlds apart." Jill remembers the two closest confidants she had as a married person. "Betty and Judy are wonderful people, but they have their children and husbands to care for."

Though they do not know it, Jack and Jill discovered the basic drive of humans. The divorce removed them both from a world they knew, one they felt comfortable in and understood. They now live in a no-man's-land, the land of the freshly singled—separated from people with whom they can relate, whether married or single.

What to do? Each settles into a livable but unfulfilling life-style. Then a friend tells Jill about a church with a special Sunday school class for single adults. "Would visiting help get me back into church?" she wonders. "I need to go at least once. The kids need to get back into a church setting. Will the other children accept them, since they come from a broken home?"

The next Sunday she takes Billy and Sally to church for the first time in a year. She finds them a class, then timidly makes her way to the one for singles. Nearing the room and hearing people laughing and talking, a fear of going in alone churns inside her. Will they act friendly toward her? After fifteen years of marriage, will she fit into this group?

To her delight, the members of the class make her feel welcome. No one gives her a funny look because she is a "divorced" woman. The men do not eye her as did the men in the night clubs but instead welcome her to the class. The ladies greet her and do not act threatened by her presence. She discovers that most of the members have experienced divorce. A few widowed and never-marrieds also belong to the class.

To her delight, Jill feels secure around the group of new acquaintances. She can now make new friends with men and women who experienced situations similar to hers. Jill feels she can now continue a church relationship with peers who are trying to build a new life, the same as she.

As the Hebrews raced toward the promised land and their future, God gave Moses and God's people a burning bush to follow at night and a cloud to guide them during the day. Singles ministries can also serve as a burning bush or glowing cloud, giving people hope and directing them to a new life. A life without pain, fear, frustration, or a lack of self-esteem.

Because Singles Ministries Heal Hurts

As you read this book, the story of Jack and Jill is happening to millions of divorced men, women, and children across the nation. Most will not be as fortunate as Jill. She enjoyed an unusual ending to her predicament—few churches have a singles program such as she found.

The isolation Jack and Jill experienced is the key to

understanding their pain. God made us to share our lives and involve ourselves with other people. Therefore, singles will continue a restless search for emotional intimacy. They will go to any lengths to find it. Erich Fromm, in his book, *The Art of Loving,* says it well:

> The deepest need of man, then, is the need to overcome his separateness, to leave the prison of his aloneness. The *absolute* failure to achieve this aim means insanity, because the panic of complete isolation can be overcome only by such a radical withdrawal from the world outside that the feeling of separation disappears—because the world outside, from which one is separated, has disappeared. (p. 8)

Divorced, widowed, and never-married persons can acutely feel this aloneness. We, as humans, need *fulfilling* contact with other people to survive as mentally healthy persons. What better place to find loving support than at a church?

Jack was less fortunate. He did not find a church to attend. Loneliness drove him to marry someone he had known for three months. The marriage lasted six months. Many singles who experience divorce or widowhood remarry prematurely. Their loneliness, being tired of living alone, and the night life drive them to make bad decisions. Others go into hibernation, severing their links with society.

Jacks and Jills probably have the lowest self-esteem of any group of people in the world. The picture of the Great American Dream begins etching itself into our minds at the moment we take our first breath. A divorce takes us out of that picture. We feel like complete failures, no longer a part of the traditional way of life.

The children—the Billys and Sallys—also can feel this painful loss of self-esteem. They do not feel worthy of their parents' love. Many ask themselves what they could have done differently to keep the marriage together. Most of these children never give up the fantasy of their parents remarrying.

This lack of self-esteem can affect *every* part of a divorced person's life, especially during the first two or three years after the marriage ends. This happens at a time when they may have to change residences, jobs, churches, income levels, and friends; they may also lose contact with family members. Men and women need time to realize they are not first-class creeps just because one part of their life did not work out. Where can they go to feel safe while that time passes? Singles ministries can provide that place. They can help people recover from this feeling of unworthiness by providing them a place to heal from the wounds of divorce or widowhood. They can help them grow into new persons by providing them with a place to worship their God.

In spite of all the pain, most singles say that this dark period in which they search for a new self is a character builder. If the much needed, healthy, supportive relationships with caring people are available, struggling to deal with the pain of a divorce or being widowed can be positive.Trying to build a new way of life on limited finances and searching for a new partner can be a growing experience. Surely, churches exist, at least in part, to heal hurts, offer God's grace, and strengthen the personal well-being of those who desire to serve God. With what other groups of people in society can such a ministry be more beneficial?

Because Singles Do Not Fit into Other Church Groups

Jesus told us to love our neighbor as ourselves (Luke 10:27). He then used the story of the Good Samaritan to define our neighbor as *anyone* who is injured whether they are our next-door neighbor, a stranger, or even our enemy (Luke 10:30-37). Even if we have only a few singles in our church, our community is full of them. Churches that serve singles are in the basic business for which all churches exist—the good-neighbor business. The classes and groups of married couples cannot effectively meet the spiritual, emotional, and social needs of most of these single neighbors.

Although Jack and Jill tried to find a church when the divorce occurred, they could not fit in. Most newly divorced persons feel uncomfortable going to Sunday school with married couples, who often look upon divorced people as losers. This attitude does not strengthen the self-esteem of a person already grieving over a broken marriage. Unless churches design a special ministry specifically for singles, they will serve very few people from this segment of society. Married people can have the world's worst relationship, but when a catastrophe hits, they pull together. If either one of them gets a raise in pay, he or she has someone who really cares. They may hate each other, but they will share the triumphs and catastrophes with each other. Bad marriages are often like the snake and mouse sitting on a log in the river during a forest fire. Although enemies in the good times, they will bond together during the bad times.

As a rule, singles lack this support. The single mother must take care of her sick children alone. She must grapple with her limited finances and make major decisions about her small family alone. The single father must face the empty apartment Sunday mornings alone. He will miss many of his children's everyday triumphs and set-backs. Most singles deal with their problems and victories alone. This is especially true if they have no family living in the area to look to for support (although this is sometimes a mixed blessing).

I learned about this basic need when I moved to Tulsa, Oklahoma, soon after my divorce. Not knowing one person in Tulsa, I craved someone to talk with. I visited a few churches, but seeing a daddy, mother, and two children bothered me—a lot. My divorce remained too fresh in my mind. (At the time, I did not even know singles ministries existed.) A supermarket not far from where I lived had a coffee shop. I can remember going there, buying a cup of coffee and a doughnut, and just sitting, watching the people shop. Exciting. Occasionally, someone would smile in my direction, which was the reason I sat there.

Looking back, I now realize that my motive was to find someone who would acknowledge that I was among the living. I was searching for something to be a part of. Finally, it dawned on me that a supermarket is not the best place to make special friends. How intimate can two people get while discussing a box of prunes?

I spent the first year and a half after my divorce without any support group. This felt more like forty months than eighteen! I finally heard about a couple of churches with singles ministries. But somehow they did not fill my needs. Now single, I wanted and needed a support group of peers.

After hearing about Phoenix, I decided to visit one Sunday morning and was pleasantly surprised by what I found. At the time, I thought the class was huge (about seventy-five singles attended each Sunday morning). Phoenix had separate classes that dealt with the single life-style and fun social events. I joined and found what I needed—a support group. My experience of being alone is no different from millions of other people who divorce or become widowed.

If churches fail to meet this need, singles will continue their restless search for intimacy, elsewhere. They will do their hunting at bars and perhaps have one-night stands. Many singles even jump into another marriage before they have dealt with the pain of their divorce or widowhood. If the church will give singles a place to worship with their peers and where they can continue their search for intimacy, they will have a much better atmosphere than the nightclubs, singles bars, and dating services. Just as important, they can rebuild their intimacy with God.

Most divorced people find their minds saturated with a lack of trust. A shattered marriage can destroy any trust that one has in members of the opposite sex. Some ask, "Why did God let this happen to me?" "If he loved me, he would not have let this happen." Widowers often ask the same questions. "Why did God take my spouse? Why do I have to live alone?"

Most newly singled persons need about two years to work through these feelings and recover their sense of trust. A male friend of mine said that five years passed before he felt comfortable as a single. Most of the people I have known spent at *least* two years getting comfortable with their life as a single person. Those who try to short-cut their recovery process often wind up in a bad marriage and must start over. Where can they go and to whom can they relate while this is happening? Singles groups are the best answer.

Singles learn how to form Platonic relationships with the

opposite sex that most married people never get to enjoy—intimate friendships that continue, even if one of the friends remarries.

I met a woman several years ago, and we started dating. After a few dates, we decided that our deepening friendship was more important than a romantic relationship, and we quit dating. She is now remarried, but our friendship remains as firm as ever. Occasionally, we still have lunch together. Her husband, having been single for several years, understands our friendship and does not feel threatened or jealous. Sometimes we invite him to eat lunch with us and sometimes we do not.

Single people will understand what I'm talking about, as will people who have remarried. The concept of men and women becoming best friends is one of the most valuable lessons, if not the most valuable, we learn after divorce. We share our troubles and our triumphs. We listen to one another, with no subject too delicate to discuss. Singles also have a unique way of being intimate with a crowd. We will notice this interesting phenomenon as our churches' singles ministry grows. Sharing our troubles and triumphs with our peers at Sunday school is rewarding and comforting. We discover that other people have similar problems. Someone else in the group has often experienced something similar and can help. This cannot happen if we try to participate in a group where everyone is married and has not experienced our kind of problems for fifteen years, if ever.

Because Singles Strengthen a Church's Effectiveness

Churches without an effective singles ministry will find it difficult to maintain a healthy, growing "Body of Christ" in our present culture. The high divorce rate is an important but usually overlooked reason for the decline in most mainline denominations. One or both of the partners who divorce usually leave the church where they worshiped together. When both partners leave, the children go too. Churches cannot stop this type of membership drain. However, they can counterbalance it by organizing a singles ministry.

Are there many Jacks and Jills for us to serve? About 50 percent of the population of the city or town in which we live are single adults. I once heard a minister say that 750,000 single adults lived within a five mile radius of the north Dallas church where he served. He speculated that less than 5 percent of them attended church with any regularity. If 1 *percent* of those singles started attending this church, the membership would increase by 7,500. Even if only one-half of 1 percent joined, there would be 3,750 new members.

Where better to learn about marriages and how to live as a single than at church? What more appropriate place to indulge positive values? What other institution is better organized to start chopping away at the tentacles of the continuing divorce plague? What better place to give the family unit a strong base from which to work?

Do some of our church leaders frown on the single life, seeing no place for it in the church's ministry? You may want to remind them gently that the world's most famous preacher and teacher lived his entire adult life as a single, Jesus.

II

Six Month Schedule Week-by-Week

We never know how high we are
Till we are called to rise
And then, if we are true to plan
Our statures touch the skies.
        —*Emily Dickinson*

Any organization, whether it be a large corporation or a singles ministry in a small town in North Dakota, needs a plan to succeed. Many singles ministries begin with enthusiasm, but after a month or so they falter and fall by the wayside. A major reason for their failure is the lack of a plan.

In this chapter we will discuss ways to structure the class, and where and when to meet. We will talk about educational plans, social activities, and other aspects that have proven successful in many ministries. The chapter is a week-by-week, twenty-six week outline. After the twenty-six weeks—or six months—merely repeat the process. Then, after your first year, you will have succeeded in building a successful singles ministry.

If your church already has a singles ministry, some of the ideas may help it to become better organized or more vital. Have faith in yourselves and in your program's future. Keep the vision of a successful ministry in focus, and it soon will become a reality.

Who do you know that might enjoy participating in a singles ministry? Use the Membership Sheet (p. 114) in the Special Forms chapter to list the singles in your church. A workable number of persons is ten to fifteen. What you need, at first, is a core group to take charge for the first few months. Starting with too many will make decision-making and planning more difficult.

Schedule a potluck dinner at someone's home, preferably on a Saturday night. The group members need to get to know one another. What better setting than at a home while eating together? The purpose of the first meeting is to choose some temporary leaders, discuss educational ideas, and schedule a few social events. The entire six months does not have to be scheduled the first night. The new leaders may feel overwhelmed at the thought of trying to plan so many educational programs and social events. How you start is not important, but how you finish is. Successful ventures rarely become that way overnight. The details will work themselves out as you go. The better foundation you lay, the better the results.

Week 1

After the potluck dinner the group members should get to know one another better. Encourage each person to tell where they work, how long they have been single, number of children, and why they want to join a singles ministry. List the reasons why everyone wants to join. The reasons will help you to make plans and give everyone a better idea of why a ministry is needed.

The attendees also need to start planning and working together, which can mean who brings what dish to the potluck. The core group will work together for the next few months. They need to let the leadership start to emerge, and it will. Many groups do not have a leader at first, but somehow one materializes.

The second purpose of the meeting is to talk about the future of the new program. People need to be aware that it will not happen overnight. Our society demands instant success. However, most ministries need from six months to a year to become a smooth-running, focused organization. Be sure to have this book at the meeting. You will need it to guide you.

Pastors should let the singles make their own decisions about their ministry. Many churches set the guidelines and make the plans. They tell the singles exactly how to run the ministry and who will run it. Do this and one probably will not be as successful. The singles must involve themselves in planning and leadership. What they need from you is support. The singles will work themselves to death for themselves. But unless they do the planning and organizing of the ministry, they will not feel as involved as they should. They will sit back and let clergy make their plans for them, which will not work for the long term. The singles need to stay within the guidelines of the church, but they still need to lead themselves.

This first night is a good time to discuss a name for the class. A definition of the name Phoenix is in the introduction, and is not trademarked. Other singles ministries have names such as Single Again, Maranatha, and Singles of Agape. The names are endless and limited only by the imagination. A name does not have to be chosen at the first meeting but do list the possibilities.

Think about selecting a motto. One motto is "Caring, Sharing, and Repairing." A successful singles ministry must care for others, enable members to share their lives with their peers, and help people repair broken lives. Your ministry needs a good balance of the three.

Decide when to have the class meeting. Most singles ministries meet on Sunday morning. People have a habit of going to Sunday school at 9:30 to 10:00. This time probably will be the best. Once you decide, leave it as is for at least two months. If the visitors are unsure of when to come, they will stay at home. Remember, most singles have left the church because of their divorce. Make it easy for them to come back.

Ask the church to assign the ministry a larger room than you think is necessary. The growth could be rapid and space will be needed for expansion. Singles ministries, properly organized, have a way of growing faster than most people expect. Without the necessary space to grow, the ministry will be stifled from the start.

Discuss, at this first meeting, educational plans and social events. A singles ministry must structure itself around educational classes *and* social events. Social events are fun and necessary, but they will not sustain the inner needs of the members. Always remember: *Fun will get them there, and education will keep them there.* Singles want to be socially active and will be drawn to activities that will enable them to mingle with other singles. Provide them with a good educational format and they will become loyal members, and the ministry will grow.

Some denominations have separate classes for the men and the women. This absolutely will not work in a singles ministry. Men and women need to learn together, worship together, and socialize together. Having coed classes will greatly benefit each sex as they rebuild their lives. A better understanding of the opposite sex will help each to have a more successful life, whether married or single. Both sexes need to hear how the other feels about different issues of life. Learning together will help men and women learn how to have Platonic relationships. Most people have never experienced this type of involvement with the opposite sex.

The Sunday morning after the potluck dinner is an excellent time to have more discussion about the future of the ministry. People will have had time to think about the previous night's meeting and may have some new ideas.

Select some temporary leadership. The volunteers do not need to commit for six months. That will come later. For now, someone needs to take charge of several areas of the ministry. Find volunteers for president, secretary and/or treasurer, social activities director, education director, and newcomers director. The rest of the officers can be chosen later. If the core group has enough members, find a volunteer for all thirteen offices.

Do not worry about inviting guests to join the ministry for at least a month. The core group members need time to do some bonding with one another. They need time to lay their groundwork and become organized. The sooner you get the machinery running, the sooner the ministry can grow efficiently. Newcomers will be more of a hindrance for the first month than an asset.

If you have time for an educational session this morning, fine. If not, do not worry about it. You need to make plans, and Sunday morning is an easy time to get the group together. Singles have a busy schedule, children to care for, and the duties of running a household alone. You can pretty well depend on having them attend Sunday morning.

The calendars included in this chapter will provide guidelines to help schedule events. Included is a sample of a planned year. You may want to personalize this schedule for your ministry. If so, just use blank calendars and then revise the activities to suit your group. *Do not schedule too many activities!* The ministry should get well organized before planning the entire calendar. New officers do not need to feel overwhelmed at trying to keep the group busy.

Decide where you want to have Sunday lunch for the next two months. On a planning calendar, list the names and addresses of the places where you will eat after church. A consistent meeting place, whether public or private, will help the newer members feel more comfortable. This will encourage them to attend more functions. Make copies and pass them out to the members. If more than six or seven people plan to attend Sunday lunch, call the restaurant and make reservations. As the ministry grows, calling ahead will become even more important. The manager may need to make arrangements so you can sit together. He may want to bring in an extra waitress, and maybe even an extra cook. Large singles ministries can swamp a restaurant.

Also, request that the waitress issue separate checks. You will have a much easier time paying the bill. Receiving separate checks also will help everyone to tip properly. Be sure to remind everyone to do so. A waitress, not properly tipped, will not look forward to seeing your group in the

CLASS ACTIVITY SCHEDULE SHEET

1. Breakfast for Eight—(B/8)
2. Christmas Party—(C/P)
3. Dinners for Eight—(D/8)
4. Divorce Adjustment Workshop—(D/A)
5. Election Sunday—(E/S)
6. Friday Fellowship—(F/F)
7. Installation Party—(I/P)
8. Lake Day—(L/D)
9. Living as a Single Workshop—(LS/W)
10. Mid-Week Study Groups—(S/G)
11. New Years Party—(N/YP)
12. Football Watch Party—(FP)
13. Newcomers Party—(NC/P)
14. Outside Trips—(O/T)
15. Pickin and Grinnin—(PG)
16. Recreation Events—(R/E)
17. Retreats—(RTS)
18. Saturday Night Live—(SNL)
19. Slave Auction—(S/A)
20. Study Groups—(S/G)
21. Sunday Lunch—(S/L)

1. JANUARY:
   First Week _____
   Second Week _____
   Third Week _____
   Fourth Week _____

2. FEBRUARY:
   First Week _____
   Second Week _____
   Third Week _____
   Fourth Week _____

3. MARCH:
   First Week _____
   Second Week _____
   Third Week _____
   Fourth Week _____

4. APRIL:
   First Week _____
   Second Week _____
   Third Week _____
   Fourth Week _____

5. MAY:
   First Week _____
   Second Week _____
   Third Week _____
   Fourth Week _____

6. JUNE:
   First Week _____
   Second Week _____
   Third Week _____
   Fourth Week _____

7. JULY:
   First Week _____
   Second Week _____
   Third Week _____
   Fourth Week _____

8. AUGUST:
   First Week _____
   Second Week _____
   Third Week _____
   Fourth Week _____

9. SEPTEMBER:
   First Week _____
   Second Week _____
   Third Week _____
   Fourth Week _____

10. OCTOBER:
   First Week _____
   Second Week _____
   Third Week _____
   Fourth Week _____

11. NOVEMBER:
   First Week _____
   Second Week _____
   Third Week _____
   Fourth Week _____

12. DECEMBER:
   First Week _____
   Second Week _____
   Third Week _____
   Fourth Week _____

CALENDAR OF EVENTS   MONTH _____   YEAR _____

SUNDAY	MONDAY	TUESDAY	WEDNESDAY	THURSDAY	FRIDAY	SATURDAY	NOTES
LUNCH 12:30					FELLOWSHIP 5:30		
LUNCH 12:30					FELLOWSHIP 5:30		
LUNCH 12:30					FELLOWSHIP 5:30		
LUNCH 12:30					FELLOWSHIP 5:30	POTLUCK DINNER	
LUNCH 12:30					FELLOWSHIP 5:30		

A. BREAKFAST FOR EIGHT
B. CHRISTMAS PARTY
C. DINNERS FOR EIGHT
D. DIVORCE ADJUSTMENT WORKSHOP
E. ELECTION SUNDAY
F. FRIDAY FELLOWSHIP
G. INSTALLATION PARTY

H. LAKE DAY
I. LIVING AS A SINGLE WORKSHOP
J. MID-WEEK SUPPORT GROUPS
K. NEW YEARS PARTY
L. NEWCOMERS PARTY
M. OUTSIDE TRIPS
N. PICKIN' N' GRINNIN'

O. RECREATION EVENTS
P. RETREATS
Q. SATURDAY NIGHT LIVE
R. SLAVE AUCTION
S. STUDY GROUPS
T. SUNDAY LUNCH

CALENDAR OF EVENTS   MONTH _____   YEAR _____

SUNDAY	MONDAY	TUESDAY	WEDNESDAY	THURSDAY	FRIDAY	SATURDAY	NOTES
LUNCH 12:30					FELLOWSHIP 5:30		
LUNCH 12:30					FELLOWSHIP 5:30	MOVIE AND PIZZA NIGHT	
LUNCH 12:30					FELLOWSHIP 5:30		
LUNCH 12:30 BOARD MEETING					FELLOWSHIP 5:30		
					FELLOWSHIP 5:30		

A. BREAKFAST FOR EIGHT
B. CHRISTMAS PARTY
C. DINNERS FOR EIGHT
D. DIVORCE ADJUSTMENT WORKSHOP
E. ELECTION SUNDAY
F. FRIDAY FELLOWSHIP
G. INSTALLATION PARTY

H. LAKE DAY
I. LIVING AS A SINGLE WORKSHOP
J. MID-WEEK SUPPORT GROUPS
K. NEW YEARS PARTY
L. NEWCOMERS PARTY
M. OUTSIDE TRIPS
N. PICKIN' N' GRINNIN'

O. RECREATION EVENTS
P. RETREATS
Q. SATURDAY NIGHT LIVE
R. SLAVE AUCTION
S. STUDY GROUPS
T. SUNDAY LUNCH

CALENDAR OF EVENTS   MONTH _____ YEAR _____

SUNDAY	MONDAY	TUESDAY	WEDNESDAY	THURSDAY	FRIDAY	SATURDAY	NOTES
LUNCH 12:30 / CHOOSE OFFICERS	CALL NEWCOMERS				FELLOWSHIP 5:30	SATURDAY NIGHT LIVE	
LUNCH 12:30	CALL NEWCOMERS				FELLOWSHIP 5:30		
LUNCH 12:30	CALL NEWCOMERS				FELLOWSHIP 5:30	DINNERS FOR EIGHT	
LUNCH 12:30 / BOARD MEETING	CALL NEWCOMERS			NEWCOMERS PARTY	FELLOWSHIP 5:30		
LUNCH 12:30	CALL NEWCOMERS				FELLOWSHIP 5:30		

A. BREAKFAST FOR EIGHT
B. CHRISTMAS PARTY
C. DINNERS FOR EIGHT
D. DIVORCE ADJUSTMENT WORKSHOP
E. ELECTION SUNDAY
F. FRIDAY FELLOWSHIP
G. INSTALLATION PARTY

H. LAKE DAY
I. LIVING AS A SINGLE WORKSHOP
J. MID-WEEK SUPPORT GROUPS
K. NEW YEARS PARTY
L. NEWCOMERS PARTY
M. OUTSIDE TRIPS
N. PICKIN' N' GRINNIN'

O. RECREATION EVENTS
P. RETREATS
Q. SATURDAY NIGHT LIVE
R. SLAVE AUCTION
S. STUDY GROUPS
T. SUNDAY LUNCH

CALENDAR OF EVENTS   MONTH _____ YEAR _____

SUNDAY	MONDAY	TUESDAY	WEDNESDAY	THURSDAY	FRIDAY	SATURDAY	NOTES
LUNCH 12:30 / SUNDAY DINNER	CALL NEWCOMERS				FELLOWSHIP 5:30	PICKIN' N' GRINNIN'	
LUNCH 12:30	CALL NEWCOMERS				FELLOWSHIP 5:30	LAKE DAY	
LUNCH 12:30 / BOARD MEETING	CALL NEWCOMERS				FELLOWSHIP 5:30		
LUNCH 12:30	CALL NEWCOMERS				FELLOWSHIP 5:30	SATURDAY NIGHT LIVE	
LUNCH 12:30	CALL NEWCOMERS				FELLOWSHIP 5:30		

A. BREAKFAST FOR EIGHT
B. CHRISTMAS PARTY
C. DINNERS FOR EIGHT
D. DIVORCE ADJUSTMENT WORKSHOP
E. ELECTION SUNDAY
F. FRIDAY FELLOWSHIP
G. INSTALLATION PARTY

H. LAKE DAY
I. LIVING AS A SINGLE WORKSHOP
J. MID-WEEK SUPPORT GROUPS
K. NEW YEARS PARTY
L. NEWCOMERS PARTY
M. OUTSIDE TRIPS
N. PICKIN' N' GRINNIN'

O. RECREATION EVENTS
P. RETREATS
Q. SATURDAY NIGHT LIVE
R. SLAVE AUCTION
S. STUDY GROUPS
T. SUNDAY LUNCH

CALENDAR OF EVENTS   MONTH _____   YEAR _____

SUNDAY	MONDAY	TUESDAY	WEDNESDAY	THURSDAY	FRIDAY	SATURDAY	NOTES
LUNCH 12:30 / NOMINATING COMMITTEE CHOSEN	CALL NEWCOMERS				FELLOWSHIP 5:30	MOVIE AND PIZZA NIGHT	
LUNCH 12:30 / NOMINATING FORMS AVAILABLE	CALL NEWCOMERS				FELLOWSHIP 5:30	BREAKFAST FOR EIGHT	
LUNCH 12:30 / NOMINATING FORMS AVAILABLE	CALL NEWCOMERS				FELLOWSHIP 5:30	SKATING PARTY	
LUNCH 12:30 / BOARD MEETS INTRODUCE CANDIDATES	CALL NEWCOMERS			NEWCOMERS PARTY	FELLOWSHIP 5:30	POTLUCK DINNER	
LUNCH 12:30	CALL NEWCOMERS				FELLOWSHIP 5:30		

A. BREAKFAST FOR EIGHT
B. CHRISTMAS PARTY
C. DINNERS FOR EIGHT
D. DIVORCE ADJUSTMENT WORKSHOP
E. ELECTION SUNDAY
F. FRIDAY FELLOWSHIP
G. INSTALLATION PARTY

H. LAKE DAY
I. LIVING AS A SINGLE WORKSHOP
J. MID-WEEK SUPPORT GROUPS
K. NEW YEARS PARTY
L. NEWCOMERS PARTY
M. OUTSIDE TRIPS
N. PICKIN' N' GRINNIN'

O. RECREATION EVENTS
P. RETREATS
Q. SATURDAY NIGHT LIVE
R. SLAVE AUCTION
S. STUDY GROUPS
T. SUNDAY LUNCH

CALENDAR OF EVENTS   MONTH_____   YEAR_____

SUNDAY	MONDAY	TUESDAY	WEDNESDAY	THURSDAY	FRIDAY	SATURDAY	NOTES
LUNCH 12:30 / INTRODUCE CANDIDATES	FELLOWSHIP / CALL NEWCOMERS				FELLOWSHIP 5:30	MOVIE AND PIZZA NIGHT	
LUNCH 12:30 / ELECTION SUNDAY	FELLOWSHIP / CALL NEWCOMERS				FELLOWSHIP 5:30	PLAN YOUR OWN PARTY	
LUNCH 12:30 / JOINT BOARD MEETING	FELLOWSHIP / CALL NEWCOMERS				FELLOWSHIP 5:30	SKATING PARTY	
LUNCH 12:30 / OFFICERS SERVE JOINTLY	FELLOWSHIP / CALL NEWCOMERS			NEWCOMERS PARTY	FELLOWSHIP 5:30	DINNERS FOR EIGHT AND AFTER PARTY	
LUNCH 12:30	FELLOWSHIP / CALL NEWCOMERS				FELLOWSHIP 5:30		

A. BREAKFAST FOR EIGHT
B. CHRISTMAS PARTY
C. DINNERS FOR EIGHT
D. DIVORCE ADJUSTMENT WORKSHOP
E. ELECTION SUNDAY
F. FRIDAY FELLOWSHIP
G. INSTALLATION PARTY

H. LAKE DAY
I. LIVING AS A SINGLE WORKSHOP
J. MID-WEEK SUPPORT GROUPS
K. NEW YEARS PARTY
L. NEWCOMERS PARTY
M. OUTSIDE TRIPS
N. PICKIN' N' GRINNIN'

O. RECREATION EVENTS
P. RETREATS
Q. SATURDAY NIGHT LIVE
R. SLAVE AUCTION
S. STUDY GROUPS
T. SUNDAY LUNCH

CALENDAR OF EVENTS   MONTH _____   YEAR _____

SUNDAY	MONDAY	TUESDAY	WEDNESDAY	THURSDAY	FRIDAY	SATURDAY	NOTES
LUNCH 12:30 / INSTALL NEW OFFICERS	FELLOWSHIP / CALL NEWCOMERS		VOLLEYBALL TENNIS STUDY GROUP		FELLOWSHIP 5:30	SATURDAY NIGHT LIVE	
LUNCH 12:30 / SUNDAY DINNER	FELLOWSHIP / CALL NEWCOMERS		VOLLEYBALL TENNIS STUDY GROUP		FELLOWSHIP 5:30	BICYCLING HIKING CAMPING	
LUNCH 12:30 / BOARD MEETS / SUNDAY DINNER	FELLOWSHIP / CALL NEWCOMERS		VOLLEYBALL TENNIS STUDY GROUP		FELLOWSHIP 5:30	MOVIE AND PIZZA NIGHT	
LUNCH 12:30 / SUNDAY DINNER	FELLOWSHIP / CALL NEWCOMERS		VOLLEYBALL TENNIS STUDY GROUP	NEWCOMERS PARTY	FELLOWSHIP 5:30	PLAN YOUR OWN PARTY	
LUNCH 12:30 / SUNDAY DINNER	FELLOWSHIP / CALL NEWCOMERS		VOLLEYBALL TENNIS STUDY GROUP		FELLOWSHIP 5:30		

A. BREAKFAST FOR EIGHT
B. CHRISTMAS PARTY
C. DINNERS FOR EIGHT
D. DIVORCE ADJUSTMENT WORKSHOP
E. ELECTION SUNDAY
F. FRIDAY FELLOWSHIP
G. INSTALLATION PARTY
H. LAKE DAY
I. LIVING AS A SINGLE WORKSHOP
J. MID-WEEK SUPPORT GROUPS
K. NEW YEARS PARTY
L. NEWCOMERS PARTY
M. OUTSIDE TRIPS
N. PICKIN' N' GRINNIN'
O. RECREATION EVENTS
P. RETREATS
Q. SATURDAY NIGHT LIVE
R. SLAVE AUCTION
S. STUDY GROUPS
T. SUNDAY LUNCH

CALENDAR OF EVENTS   MONTH _____   YEAR _____

SUNDAY	MONDAY	TUESDAY	WEDNESDAY	THURSDAY	FRIDAY	SATURDAY	NOTES
LUNCH 12:30 SUNDAY DINNER	FELLOWSHIP CALL NEWCOMERS		BRIDGE VOLLEYBALL TENNIS STUDY GROUP		FELLOWSHIP 5:30	PICKIN' N' GRINNIN'	
LUNCH 12:30 SUNDAY DINNER	FELLOWSHIP CALL NEWCOMERS		BRIDGE VOLLEYBALL TENNIS STUDY GROUP		FELLOWSHIP 5:30	SKATING PARTY	
LUNCH 12:30 BOARD MEETS SUNDAY DINNER	FELLOWSHIP CALL NEWCOMERS		BRIDGE VOLLEYBALL TENNIS STUDY GROUP		FELLOWSHIP 5:30	ZOO DAY MOVIE NIGHT	
LUNCH 12:30 SUNDAY DINNER	FELLOWSHIP CALL NEWCOMERS		BRIDGE VOLLEYBALL TENNIS STUDY GROUP	NEWCOMERS PARTY	FELLOWSHIP 5:30	DINNERS FOR EIGHT AND AFTER PARTY	
LUNCH 12:30 SUNDAY DINNER	FELLOWSHIP CALL NEWCOMERS		BRIDGE VOLLEYBALL TENNIS STUDY GROUP		FELLOWSHIP 5:30		

A. BREAKFAST FOR EIGHT
B. CHRISTMAS PARTY
C. DINNERS FOR EIGHT
D. DIVORCE ADJUSTMENT WORKSHOP
E. ELECTION SUNDAY
F. FRIDAY FELLOWSHIP
G. INSTALLATION PARTY

H. LAKE DAY
I. LIVING AS A SINGLE WORKSHOP
J. MID-WEEK SUPPORT GROUPS
K. NEW YEARS PARTY
L. NEWCOMERS PARTY
M. OUTSIDE TRIPS
N. PICKIN' N' GRINNIN'

O. RECREATION EVENTS
P. RETREATS
Q. SATURDAY NIGHT LIVE
R. SLAVE AUCTION
S. STUDY GROUPS
T. SUNDAY LUNCH

CALENDAR OF EVENTS   MONTH _____   YEAR _____

SUNDAY	MONDAY	TUESDAY	WEDNESDAY	THURSDAY	FRIDAY	SATURDAY	NOTES
LUNCH 12:30 / SUNDAY DINNER	FELLOWSHIP / CALL NEWCOMERS		BRIDGE / VOLLEYBALL TENNIS STUDY GROUP		FELLOWSHIP 5:30	SATURDAY NIGHT LIVE	
LUNCH 12:30 / SUNDAY DINNER	FELLOWSHIP / CALL NEWCOMERS		BRIDGE / VOLLEYBALL TENNIS STUDY GROUP		FELLOWSHIP 5:30	MOVIE AND PIZZA NIGHT	
LUNCH 12:30 / BOARD MEETS / SUNDAY DINNER	FELLOWSHIP / CALL NEWCOMERS		BRIDGE / VOLLEYBALL TENNIS STUDY GROUP		FELLOWSHIP 5:30	OUTDOOR DAY / PLAN YOUR OWN NIGHT	
LUNCH 12:30 / SUNDAY DINNER	FELLOWSHIP / CALL NEWCOMERS		BRIDGE / VOLLEYBALL TENNIS STUDY GROUP	NEWCOMERS PARTY	FELLOWSHIP 5:30	SLAVE AUCTION	
LUNCH 12:30 / SUNDAY DINNER	FELLOWSHIP / CALL NEWCOMERS		BRIDGE / VOLLEYBALL TENNIS STUDY GROUP		FELLOWSHIP 5:30		

A. BREAKFAST FOR EIGHT
B. CHRISTMAS PARTY
C. DINNERS FOR EIGHT
D. DIVORCE ADJUSTMENT WORKSHOP
E. ELECTION SUNDAY
F. FRIDAY FELLOWSHIP
G. INSTALLATION PARTY

H. LAKE DAY
I. LIVING AS A SINGLE WORKSHOP
J. MID-WEEK SUPPORT GROUPS
K. NEW YEARS PARTY
L. NEWCOMERS PARTY
M. OUTSIDE TRIPS
N. PICKIN' N' GRINNIN'

O. RECREATION EVENTS
P. RETREATS
Q. SATURDAY NIGHT LIVE
R. SLAVE AUCTION
S. STUDY GROUPS
T. SUNDAY LUNCH

CALENDAR OF EVENTS   MONTH_____   YEAR_____

SUNDAY	MONDAY	TUESDAY	WEDNESDAY	THURSDAY	FRIDAY	SATURDAY	NOTES
LUNCH 12:30 SUNDAY DINNER	FELLOWSHIP CALL NEWCOMERS		BRIDGE VOLLEYBALL TENNIS STUDY GROUP		FELLOWSHIP 5:30	BREAKFAST FOR EIGHT DAY OUTING	
LUNCH 12:30 SUNDAY DINNER	FELLOWSHIP CALL NEWCOMERS		BRIDGE VOLLEYBALL TENNIS STUDY GROUP		FELLOWSHIP 5:30	RETREAT SKATING PARTY	
LUNCH 12:30 BOARD MEETS SUNDAY DINNER	FELLOWSHIP CALL NEWCOMERS		BRIDGE VOLLEYBALL TENNIS STUDY GROUP		FELLOWSHIP 5:30	SATURDAY NIGHT LIVE	
LUNCH 12:30 SUNDAY DINNER	FELLOWSHIP CALL NEWCOMERS		BRIDGE VOLLEYBALL TENNIS STUDY GROUP	NEWCOMERS PARTY	FELLOWSHIP 5:30	PLAN YOUR OWN PARTY	
LUNCH 12:30 SUNDAY DINNER	FELLOWSHIP CALL NEWCOMERS		BRIDGE VOLLEYBALL TENNIS STUDY GROUP		FELLOWSHIP 5:30		

A. BREAKFAST FOR EIGHT
B. CHRISTMAS PARTY
C. DINNERS FOR EIGHT
D. DIVORCE ADJUSTMENT WORKSHOP
E. ELECTION SUNDAY
F. FRIDAY FELLOWSHIP
G. INSTALLATION PARTY

H. LAKE DAY
I. LIVING AS A SINGLE WORKSHOP
J. MID-WEEK SUPPORT GROUPS
K. NEW YEARS PARTY
L. NEWCOMERS PARTY
M. OUTSIDE TRIPS
N. PICKIN' N' GRINNIN'

O. RECREATION EVENTS
P. RETREATS
Q. SATURDAY NIGHT LIVE
R. SLAVE AUCTION
S. STUDY GROUPS
T. SUNDAY LUNCH

CALENDAR OF EVENTS   MONTH _____   YEAR _____

SUNDAY	MONDAY	TUESDAY	WEDNESDAY	THURSDAY	FRIDAY	SATURDAY	NOTES
LUNCH 12:30 / NOMINATING COMMITTEE INTRODUCED	FELLOWSHIP / CALL NEWCOMERS		BRIDGE / VOLLEYBALL TENNIS STUDY GROUP		FELLOWSHIP 5:30	DIVORCE ADJUSTMENT GROUP	
LUNCH 12:30 / NOMINATING FORMS AVAILABLE	FELLOWSHIP / CALL NEWCOMERS		BRIDGE / VOLLEYBALL TENNIS STUDY GROUP		FELLOWSHIP 5:30	MOVIE AND PIZZA NIGHT	
LUNCH 12:30 / BOARD MEETS NOMINATING FORMS AVAIL	FELLOWSHIP / CALL NEWCOMERS		BRIDGE / VOLLEYBALL TENNIS STUDY GROUP		FELLOWSHIP 5:30	PICKIN' N' GRINNIN'	
LUNCH 12:30 / INTRODUCE CANDIDATES DINNER	FELLOWSHIP / CALL NEWCOMERS		BRIDGE / VOLLEYBALL TENNIS STUDY GROUP	NEWCOMERS PARTY	FELLOWSHIP 5:30	PLAN YOUR OWN PARTY	
LUNCH 12:30 / SUNDAY DINNER	FELLOWSHIP / CALL NEWCOMERS		VOLLEYBALL TENNIS STUDY GROUP		FELLOWSHIP 5:30		

A. BREAKFAST FOR EIGHT
B. CHRISTMAS PARTY
C. DINNERS FOR EIGHT
D. DIVORCE ADJUSTMENT WORKSHOP
E. ELECTION SUNDAY
F. FRIDAY FELLOWSHIP
G. INSTALLATION PARTY

H. LAKE DAY
I. LIVING AS A SINGLE WORKSHOP
J. MID-WEEK SUPPORT GROUPS
K. NEW YEARS PARTY
L. NEWCOMERS PARTY
M. OUTSIDE TRIPS
N. PICKIN' N' GRINNIN'

O. RECREATION EVENTS
P. RETREATS
Q. SATURDAY NIGHT LIVE
R. SLAVE AUCTION
S. STUDY GROUPS
T. SUNDAY LUNCH

CALENDAR OF EVENTS   MONTH _____   YEAR _____

SUNDAY	MONDAY	TUESDAY	WEDNESDAY	THURSDAY	FRIDAY	SATURDAY	NOTES
LUNCH 12:30 — INTRODUCE CANDIDATES DINNER	FELLOWSHIP — CALL NEWCOMERS		VOLLEYBALL TENNIS STUDY GROUP		FELLOWSHIP 5:30	SATURDAY OUTDOORS ACTIVITY	
LUNCH 12:30 — ELECTION SUNDAY DINNER	FELLOWSHIP — CALL NEWCOMERS		VOLLEYBALL TENNIS STUDY GROUP		FELLOWSHIP 5:30	HOME MADE ICE-CREAM & CAKE NITE	
LUNCH 12:30 — JOINT BOARD MEETING DINNER	FELLOWSHIP — CALL NEWCOMERS		VOLLEYBALL TENNIS STUDY GROUP		FELLOWSHIP 5:30	PLAN YOUR OWN PARTY	
LUNCH 12:30 — OFFICERS SERVE JOINTLY	FELLOWSHIP — CALL NEWCOMERS		VOLLEYBALL TENNIS STUDY GROUP	NEWCOMERS PARTY	FELLOWSHIP 5:30	DINNERS FOR EIGHT AND AFTER PARTY	
LUNCH 12:30 — SUNDAY DINNER	FELLOWSHIP — CALL NEWCOMERS		VOLLEYBALL TENNIS STUDY GROUP		FELLOWSHIP 5:30		

A. BREAKFAST FOR EIGHT
B. CHRISTMAS PARTY
C. DINNERS FOR EIGHT
D. DIVORCE ADJUSTMENT WORKSHOP
E. ELECTION SUNDAY
F. FRIDAY FELLOWSHIP
G. INSTALLATION PARTY

H. LAKE DAY
I. LIVING AS A SINGLE WORKSHOP
J. MID-WEEK SUPPORT GROUPS
K. NEW YEARS PARTY
L. NEWCOMERS PARTY
M. OUTSIDE TRIPS
N. PICKIN' 'N' GRINNIN'

O. RECREATION EVENTS
P. RETREATS
Q. SATURDAY NIGHT LIVE
R. SLAVE AUCTION
S. STUDY GROUPS
T. SUNDAY LUNCH

future. A restaurant manager asked Phoenix not to come back for this reason. Embarrassed is not the word for how we felt. Also, plan a fellowship time for Friday, either after work or later in the evening. Plan this event for the next two months. If you have fellowship time at someone's home, you probably will need to change homes each week. A better way is to make plans to meet at a public place for the first two months or so. Going to the same place will help attendance. This is more important for newcomers than for the regular members. People will invariably lose the calendar and forget where to go. While scheduling, ask the group if they would like to plan a Saturday night event or two. Keep this simple, such as Pizza and Movie nights. Bigger events can wait for at least two months. By then, you will have enough members to arrange a Dinners for Eight.

Plan the educational lessons for the next few months. You must have good lessons on Sunday mornings. The fellowship is fine, but people also require continuing education and religious feeding. Find a volunteer to teach for the next month or two. The resource list on p. 135 may help to choose a book the class would like to study. Teach the book by mingling a Christian theme with the author's ideas.

Schedule a board meeting for the fourth week. The leaders should start having a monthly session to discuss the progress of the ministry. They also will plan social events for the coming months. How far the ministry has progressed after each month will surprise you. The temporary officers may want to make some corrections for events already scheduled.

So, after this first week, you will schedule Sunday Lunches, Friday Fellowships, and a Movie and Pizza night. Keep the social events simple, ones that do not require much planning. You also will select an educational format. You are on your way!

Week 2

Begin now to plan for some newcomers. Though it is better not to try to find visitors at this point, some may come. Set up a newcomers' table with nametags, calendars, and someone to welcome the newcomers and sign them in. Find a volunteer to take care of the sign-in table for the next two months. Newcomers will enjoy seeing the same familiar face at the door. Remember that newcomers may be newly divorced and hurting. You can count on their shyness over visiting a singles ministry. Many will not have much self-esteem, and will be unsure of how the ministry will accept them. Greet them with a smile, and let them know that they are welcome.

Begin this session by asking if anyone in the core group has new ideas or questions. Spend some additional time, all morning if necessary, talking about the ministry's future. If any time is left over, have a little open discussion. Some possible topics are the single life-style, relationship skills, or whatever is of interest to the group.

Week 3

Start talking about dates and places for the Christmas party and New Year's party. Schedule these a year in advance, especially if you live in a large city. The board can make an educated guess about how much space the party will require. If you wait until October to make reservations, most places probably will have already reserved their banquet rooms.

The activities calendar ("Calendar of Events" sheet) within this chapter is an easy reference to suggested events. After reproducing it, put initials in the appropriate box of the month to be scheduled. For example, the Christmas Party is (CP), second on the list of options. Put this in December on the date when it will take place. Schedule the special events first. Then go back and plan the more common ones.

Week 4

Have your first board meeting and schedule one for each coming month. Plan where to have these meetings, what day, and what time they will begin. Encourage the board members to attend each meeting and arrive on time. Most singles have relatively flexible schedules. If they know that the board meetings start at a certain time, they will be there. Otherwise you might not have the attendance necessary to have an efficient meeting. This must not happen. The leaders need to feel organized and committed. If the board members are not consistent in their efforts, the new ministry will fail.

The last week of the month is a good time for board meetings. Plan the up-coming month's calendar at this meeting. The board needs to coordinate events so that there are no conflicts. After the meeting, the secretary will make copies of the calendar. Send them to everyone on your mailing list. If you use the church's non-profit mailing permit, you can save money on postage. This allows you to mail calendars and/or newsletters for about $15 per hundred (non-profit permits require not less than 200 copies in each mailing).

The president should never make reports for an absent officer. Let the officers know that their part of the board meetings will not be done unless they attend. If officers do not do their jobs, take the steps outlined in the bylaws to replace them. Of course, every rule has its exceptions. Illness, a death in the family, or work schedule changes can occur. Obviously, people cannot miss work to attend a Sunday school class board meeting. But what if the officers think they simply have something better to do? Staying home to watch a favorite TV show or having a date does not qualify as a good excuse. Each member of the board needs to feel committed to his or her job. If people cannot commit, then they should turn their duties over to someone who will.

The bylaws cover this area specifically. Though they may sound harsh—especially in a church setting—the officers guidelines must be publicized and enforced. This ensures that everyone knows the rules from the beginning. Each officer needs to have a job description, know it in advance, and be expected to fulfill his or her duties. If an officer does not take care of his or her duties, the rest of the board cannot properly take care of its responsibilities. Most social events require planning from more than one officer. If an officer is absent, something will be left undone and the group becomes disorganized.

Encourage the president to let the other officers do their jobs in their own way. When people have freedom and responsibility to fulfill their duties, they will do excellent work. New and better ideas will emerge that will benefit the class. Independently responsible officers will develop and exercise far more creativity than if the president is trying to administer everything. Give people a job to do, and get out of the way. You will love the results. They will grow and learn, and the entire program will benefit. If a president tries to be the dominant officer, he or she will soon stifle the entire program.

Start inviting a few new people to the class. Also, pass out some prospect lists to the members and plan some newcomer drives. New people also can add names to the lists. Most singles know other singles, and they can invite them to Sunday school. A core group of ten to fifteen probably can generate fifty to seventy-five prospective members. Of course, not all will wish to attend, but they cannot make a decision until they are invited. Constantly adding names to the ministries' prospect lists will ensure steady growth.

Keep the church office informed of your progress and plans. Be sure the staff always has a current calendar available. Once people outside the church hear about the ministry, the office will receive calls asking about it. The office also can alert you to singles who visit the church services.

Week 5

If the class functions are not well attended, ask the members why. Adjustments in the events are much easier to make as you go along. Do not wait until the ministry gets bogged down because the members are not enjoying the social events or the educational sessions.

Find a company that makes permanent name tags. Firms

specialize in such items at a cost of around $3.50 each. Each member is to pay for his or her own. Some groups prefer hard plastic ones 1½" × 2", which come in three separate colors. Regular members might wear a burnt orange tag with black lettering. The current officers might have a blue tag with white lettering. Past presidents could have a gold one with black lettering. This bonding adds a special touch of class to the group. The secretary is in charge of ordering the tags.

To easily identify the newcomers, supply them with yellow paper name tags. As time passes and the group grows, easy recognition of newcomers becomes more important. They will not be hard to spot when the group is small.

The person in charge of newcomers should select two or three volunteers to telephone the visitors. The callers should thank them for coming, invite them to come back, and ask them for comments about how they liked the class. Their input will help you get a feel for how the ministry is doing. If too many visit and do not come back, something is wrong. Without newcomers, the ministry will never grow. Some may decide not to come back and will let you know this. Whoever is doing the calling needs to ask them why. If you consistently get the same answers, you will want to make some adjustments.

The newcomers will appreciate the call and will be more likely to join. They want and need to feel special. After two or three months, you will have compiled a substantial list of prospective members. You also may put some of these on the mailing list.

If you planned a Dinners for Eight for the eighth week, have a sign-up sheet available on this Sunday. One will be needed for participants and one for hosts. Have the lists available for the next two weeks.

Week 6

You may hear, as the ministry grows, that if the group gets too large it will lose its intimacy. To a certain extent, this is true. A hundred members cannot have the same intimacy as will a group of ten to fifteen. As the growth continues, small groups of friends will form in the larger group. Many people call these cliques, but this is perfectly normal socialization. As new members join the group, they will find a handful of people whom they can relate to better than they can with others. This is good. People need the personal intimacy that can only come from a smaller group. Members and visitors may talk about the cliques. Do not try to do anything about this.

Maintain a filing cabinet in the church office for the singles program. Keep bulletins, board meeting minutes, and membership lists in it. Singles will come and go. If an officer should leave the program unexpectedly, all of his or her materials will be available to the class. If the officers have to keep their records at home, some will eventually get misplaced.

As your membership grows, the organizational structure will become something more than a traditional Sunday school class. The ministry will have bylaws, its own bank account, and newsletter. Become organized in ways that can sustain a large group. As the ministry grows, you can expand the number of officers and meeting rooms as needed. By properly preparing, the growth will continue uninterrupted.

Get the organization set, and growth will follow. This is exactly where most groups fail. They let the structure stay behind the growth. Plan properly and you will not have this problem.

I had a donkey, Jennifer, when I was a kid. If her head was pointed north, the tail was sure to follow. Occasionally, she would get confused and try to bite her tail, and we would start going in circles. If you do not keep structure ahead of the growth, the ministry will do a Jennifer routine.

Week 7

By now, twenty-five to fifty members could be attending each Sunday. The size of the town or city you live in will determine this. If you live in a large city, the attendance could be much greater.

Growth in new groups will stagnate occasionally. If you continue to make newcomer calls and maintain records, the stagnation will not last long. Remember, this is a planned, not haphazard, growth.

As the ministry grows, the other members of the church may talk about "all those singles." Be patient and understanding with them. Something different from the norm is happening. Married people may feel threatened or intimidated by the large growth of singles that is taking place. Some married members may feel that the singles are invading and trying to take over the church. These territorial concerns are inevitable. Pastors should continually say how proud they are of the singles. Let the rest of the church know that they also should be proud of having a special place for singles to worship. "Except for the Grace of God, there go I."

Encourage the singles to join the church choir and teach other classes in the church. Many will feel the church has become family and a home away from home. Since they are part of the church family, they will want to help all they can. Make this a positive and contributing group, and everything will be okay. The married members who may have had doubts will become accustomed to what is happening. They will adjust to the new energetic, vibrant group within the church.

Week 8

This is the week for your Dinners for Eight social. Hosts should not concern themselves about the size of their homes or apartments. One woman had dinner for twenty people in her efficiency apartment. Some ate their meal standing up, while others sat on the floor. A couple of people ate sitting on the edge of her bathtub. We had a wonderful dinner and a definite sense of togetherness. We found it impossible not to talk to one another. When you stand nose to nose and eat with someone you do not know, it is difficult to remain strangers.

A few people who attend the social events will not come to class on Sunday morning. Some visitors may attend the social events with the wrong intentions. These people will soon fall by the wayside because of the nature of the group. Be aware that this may happen occasionally. Then, too, some will attend Sunday morning activities and never attend social functions.

You will have the best Sunday morning attendance after a Dinners for Eight. People will have made new friends, and they will be looking forward to seeing them again the next morning. Having made new friends and seeing familiar faces will make everyone feel more comfortable in class. A sense of togetherness that is wonderful to watch and experience will waft its way through your membership.

People will come to the president with new ideas for the class. Some will be good, and some not so good. However, the president should always acknowledge that the idea has merit. He or she should then send the person with the idea to the appropriate officer. For example, if someone has a new idea for education, the president should send that person to the education director. Sometimes they will go, and sometimes not. Let the person with the idea decide whether to follow through. This will give him or her a choice and the responsibility of following through.

The education director should listen and make his or her own decision. If the new idea requires a major decision that will affect the entire class, present it to the board. The education director should not simply ignore the idea. Your board does not need to get a "closed-minded" reputation. Such an attitude will hinder the creativity of the class. Many excellent ideas will come from the class members. The officers—working in isolation—can get so involved in everyday duties that their creativity may suffer from low energy.

Always take any new ideas that concern the class to the board. This gives everyone the opportunity for input. The board can discuss the ideas and make decisions. This is not the president's job. *Your singles program must not become a one-person show.* A one-person leadership soon becomes a one-person ministry.

Week 9

Continue calling newcomers, and call on those who have stopped attending. Let them know you missed them and would love to have them visit again. Tell them the ministry needs their help and input. Ask them why they stopped attending. You may discover that something minor caused them not to come back. Maybe no one made them feel welcome, or they objected to the educational material. If they hedge about answering questions, do not let your feelings be hurt. Just let them know that you would love to have them come back. You cannot meet all the needs of all the people. But stay open to making corrections as the ministry progresses.

This is especially true during the first year of this program. People need a place to worship, and you can provide them with one that is unique. A member of Phoenix called me the first week I attended a singles group. The call made me feel welcome and wanted, which was the main reason I went back. Someone sounded as if they cared at a time when I needed someone to care.

Week 10

The most popular social events with the group will become clear. Various ministries will enjoy different events. Your ministry may like something different from one in another part of the country. The social events listed in this manual are merely guidelines for consideration.

Use the largest room the church has available for the Sunday morning assembly. Always set up about 25 percent

THE VITAL SINGLES MINISTRY

THE VITAL SINGLES MINISTRY

more chairs than you think you will need. This does two things. First, it makes the class aware that it has room to grow. We experimented with the number of chairs set up for Phoenix meetings. The 25-percent-extra-chair rule works. If 250 people attended one Sunday morning, I would ask the custodian to set up 315 chairs for the next Sunday. The idea of the goldfish bowl works. Fish will multiply to fill the size of their space. Your group will do the same. Give fish a small bowl, and you get fewer new fish. An organization will only fill a room to the amount of space available. Your singles ministry needs enough room to grow.

The second reason is equally important. If newcomers cannot find a place to sit, they may not come back. They will feel uncomfortable standing and think they look conspicuous. Visitors to your program probably will be shy at first. Most people, especially after a divorce, have a difficult time reaching out to make new friends. In a foreign environment, they probably will feel uncomfortable. Newcomers will be more relaxed if they can sit without anyone noticing them.

Week 11

Make sure that your calling committee continues diligently. We keep repeating this because it is important. Word of mouth also will spread the news of your ministry. When you couple this with constant newcomer calling, the ministry will grow rapidly. Stay prepared for an explosion of growth, which can happen unexpectedly through a surge of newcomers. If you do not prepare, growth will be slower than it could be. Remember the donkey that goes in circles.

Some visitors feel comfortable in a United Methodist church, and some feel more relaxed in a Southern Baptist setting. This is just the way of North American denominational preference. Thus we have another reason to be persistent in calling newcomers. Give them an opportunity to make choices to meet their needs.

Week 12

Your new singles ministry is now three months old. A feeling of comradeship and enthusiasm for the group will be stronger than ever before. The members will be having fun socially and enjoying their church life more. You will see the singles grow and become more confident. After all, this is what the group is all about.

Church membership also will start to show new growth because of the singles. The ministry will attract more new members than you ever thought possible. The singles may make up the majority of the visitors and new members.

Week 13

By now, you have a handle on the purpose of your particular singles ministry. Continue the basics. Maintain your calling committee, continue to plan future events, and keep the educational program interesting.

Persistence is the key. Do not relax your work habits, or the growth of the ministry may lapse. In the future, membership will start to grow almost by its own will. When this happens, you will know you have done your homework. Wait until after the first year before you consider relaxing. By then, the ministry will have become an excellent, smooth functioning organization—but you are not there yet.

So far, we have covered three months of planning and organizing your new singles ministry. The information that has made many singles ministries successful is outlined for those first twelve weeks. Be creative and flexible, and choose events as the need arises.

Once you begin a schedule, stay with it. The reason most plans do not work is that they are not followed. Your church may be small and unable to use the entire structure. If so, the book will be a source for adaptation. However, the ideas for enjoyable social events and educational programs are still appropriate.

Week 14

Design your own week. Use the preceding calendars to decide what type of activities you want. This is a good time to ask the officers to create some new social activities and educational ideas.

The president and vice-president should now decide who they want to serve on the nominating committee. The ratio of officers and class members is important. The present officers on the nominating committee have the experience to know what type of person is necessary for each office. The class members probably will know more members than do the officers. Regular class members on the nominating committee will keep the board from becoming too centralized. Church politics can be ugly. The class members should feel they have more say about who their leaders will be than does the board. This is absolutely necessary. The opposite can hurt.

Select a combination of men and women to serve on the committee. Keep the ratio as nearly equal as possible. This ensures that both sexes have an equal say about the nominees.

Week 15

The president and the vice-president will complete the nominating committee. The nominating committee is to choose a chairperson. He or she may be a board member or a class member.

Week 16

Introduce the nominating committee to the class. The chairperson declares that the committee is taking nominations for new officers. He or she will state the guidelines for recommending someone. Each of the ones listed below has a definite purpose.

(1) Nominees must be members of the class.
(2) Nominees must be members of your church.
(3) Nominees must know of their nomination and sign a nomination form. (A sample is in the Special Forms chapter.)
(4) Nominees should be reasonably certain they can serve a full term of office.
(5) Nominees for president must have served on a previous board. They must have attended at least four board meetings (this rule will not be possible the first year). People need to prove themselves in leadership before becoming a president. Being a captain of industry does not make you a good singles leader.

Having a presidential candidate who has served on a previous board will serve two objectives: (1) That person will have learned the workings of the class. (2) The rest of the class and the board will have had a chance to watch the candidate's leadership style.

Week 17

The nominating committee members will set up a special table and stock it with nominating forms. The committee should not rely strictly on volunteers to serve as officers. They also should actively seek those who they feel will make good officers. Be sure to ask potential officers to decide in which office they would like to serve. One person might enjoy being party director more than secretary. If the officers lack enthusiasm for their duties, their terms will seem long and endless.

Week 18

The nominating committee will make nomination forms available to the class. Every Sunday the chairperson announces the offices still needing candidates. Committee members should make telephone calls to be sure everyone has an opportunity to serve.

Though often feeling they lack the ability, many singles may resist leadership roles. Self-esteem problems due to divorce may be a reason. By asking them to serve as an officer of the class, we will boost their egos. Many of the best officers have to have their arms twisted a little before they agree to serve.

Week 19

This is the Sunday to introduce the slate of officers to the class. Have the chairperson of the nominating committee introduce each candidate. If possible, have two candidates for each office. Sometimes this is not practical, especially in the beginning of your ministry. However, the elections will have an element of fun if two or more candidates run for each office.

Week 20

Introduce the candidates to the class again. Allow each to give a brief campaign speech if they wish. Set a time limit of two minutes for each. At first, this will not be as important as it will be later. The time will come when you have a full slate of officers. If each candidate speaks for two minutes, it will take thirty minutes of class time. Do not worry about this. These officers will serve for the next six months. A little time spent preparing will be worth the effort.

Most of the class members will not attend every Sunday morning. Some will have their children and prefer to be with them. Others will prefer to sleep in because their children are gone for the weekend. As your ministry grows, you will find that about one-third of the members will attend each week. This is the reason for introducing the candidates for three consecutive Sunday mornings.

Week 21

Election Sunday is the third Sunday before the new officers take office. Consider suspending classes and serving coffee and donuts. This will enable the class members to mingle and get to know one another better.

The nominating committee will have ballots available, a sample of which is in the Special Forms chapter. Distribute the ballots to the members of the class. Ask the visitors not to vote. (Easy identification of membership status is another good reason for the different colored name tags.)

The nominating committee will collect the completed ballots and go to a separate room to count them. While the ballots are being counted, the class members might want to have small group discussions on a special subject chosen by the education director. Make Election Sunday a fun day. You have six months to be serious and follow a schedule.

Week 22

The out-going and in-coming officers will have a joint meeting today. This gives the new board members a chance to observe a planning session. The present officers can further explain the duties of their respective offices. Do not skip this meeting! The new officers need to know as much as possible about their duties.

Week 23

The in-coming and out-going officers will serve together today. The new officers will have the chance for hands-on experience. Elections are over, and it is time to resume normal class functions.

THE VITAL SINGLES MINISTRY

Week 24

This Saturday night, have the installation celebration. Schedule a Dinners for Eight and have everyone come together for an after dinner party. Have a break during the party and present the new officers. *Please give special recognition to the out-going officers.* This acknowledgment of their commitment to the class is their only pay check for their efforts. Install the new officers the next morning so the whole class can observe the installation. Some of them will not have attended the party.

Week 25

Install your new officers and let them take charge this morning. Be sure to recognize again the out-going board. They have worked hard and will appreciate some recognition.

The out-going president will install the new officers. They need to feel something more than the weight of an officer's badge. The new board members need to feel committed and responsible for the next six months. Below is a suggested oath of office:

I, (name), do hereby accept the office of (name of office). I agree to fulfill the duties of (name of office) to the best of my ability. I will observe the bylaws of (class name). I will always keep the (class name) needs uppermost in my mind. I will perform my duties in a Christian manner, always keeping the (church name) and the (class name) objectives as my guidelines. I will attempt to improve my office in at least one area during my term. I am always open to new ideas that will make (class name) a better ministry for singles.

The new idea statement will help remind the new officers always to search for ways to improve the class. Any organization can become lax in developing new ideas. Always seek new ways to improve the class. The more sparkle you can give your ministry, the more successful it will

72

become. Trying to give a church organization "sparkle" sounds strange, but it is okay to have fun at church.

Huge changes make people nervous. Little improvements, as the ministry grows, will stimulate the members' interest and keep them coming in the door. A steady and continuing growth will ensure that the ministry will always be there when needed. If you get too set in the old methods, the ministry will become stale and boring.

Week 26

Several years ago, I consulted for a small church wanting to start a singles ministry. The pastor had appointed four married couples as sponsors. He had also asked a never-married man to be the singles leader. The man believed that all divorced people were sinners and possibly awaiting God's judgment. He objected to every point I was trying to make to help their ministry.

During a question and answer session, my associate pointed out that I should address the issues of sex and booze. The second she said that, two of the married couples got up and left through the door. You would have thought the church was on fire. At that point, I almost wished it were, so I also could leave. The single people in the audience did not even flinch, except the leader. His eyeballs almost popped out onto the floor. Her statement stunned him into silence for the first time (a blessing from above). My associate was not trying to be cynical or offensive. She merely wanted to point out two key issues of which churches must be aware.

Whether church members, deacons, pastors, or anyone else likes it or not, singles are sexual beings. Romances will blossom and couples will make choices. Most religions and denominations preach against sex outside marriage. The Bible speaks of adultery and fornication. To pass judgment on this issue is not my purpose. This issue, however, must be discussed, because the subject will surface among the singles and church members.

As Erich Fromm stated in *The Art of Loving*, "People need to be a part of another person. The joining of two people can be mental and/or physical." Singles may have sex merely to be touched by another human. I learned the accuracy of Fromm's statement in a very personal story.

After my wife and I legally separated, the divorce did not occur for almost nine months. During that time, I was busy and moving to Tulsa. I hardly even talked to a woman during that nine-month period.

The divorce became final. As a single one of my dates turned into a one-night stand. She and I had not even met before that night. Sex was the last thing I was looking for at that point in my life. I remember the tender touch of another person. The touching was wonderful, and in no way do I refer to the sexual contact. Sex had nothing to do with that night. She apparently needed some tenderness and touching as much as I did. We happened to meet when we both had the same need.

That night will always have a special place in my memory. The drive we all have to be touched and held by another person was our compelling motivation. Millions of singles could tell the same story. This need is indicative of the restless search for intimacy that is described in chapter one.

Jesus plainly says, "Do not judge, so that you may not be judged" (Matthew 7:1). Remember this as your ministry begins to grow. The singles will not embarrass you. However, some church members may take issue with the hugging and touching among the singles. The majority of this physical contact you see at the church will be platonic.

Why do most members of singles ministries do a lot of hugging? Many of them do not have any hugs or touching during the week. Psychiatrists can prove that we all need a certain amount of touching to be mentally healthy. Without contact we become depressed and out of sorts with the world. I can still remember the day after my one-night stand. I felt contented and at peace with myself. My outlook on life was better than it had been for months.

Many articles and books have been written about being a "whole person" and not needing another person to be happy. In many ways this is true. Singles can and do lead productive lives by themselves—some do as celibates. However, unless they have someone special in their lives, most people are not completely whole. A niche exists in each of us that is empty without tenderness and touching. This is the reason I felt so good the day after. That niche was filled, if only temporarily. Singles constantly will search for intimacy.

The next issue is alcohol, which rarely presents a problem for singles ministries. But in any large group of people, some will drink. This is not a problem for most ministries, but someone occasionally will bring alcohol to a party. Some singles turn to drink after they divorce. However, the members of your ministry need to know that drinking is not allowed at the parties. Approach the problem positively, and the singles will respect your position.

The larger your ministry becomes, the more these two issues—sex and alcohol—will arise. Be understanding and considerate of the singles. The greatest problems will likely be in the minds of those who are judgmental. Each church and denomination must handle this according to its own understanding of Christian teaching. But you are now aware of what will arise.

Another piece of advice about your singles ministry that is easily forgotten: Go "first class" at every opportunity. If you have dances, have them at the most expensive place you can afford. The cost probably will not be that much greater than having the event at an apartment clubhouse. An extra dollar admission per person can go a long way toward creating a first-class evening. Many singles cannot afford to go to really nice places. In most cases mothers are raising their children on one paycheck, and fathers are paying child support. If you have special social events occasionally, people will appreciate it. They will have a chance to put on their evening clothes and enjoy an evening of elegance.

Try to keep admission to social events below $5 per person. Once you have 100 to 200 people attending, $5 goes a long way toward a pleasant evening. Do not try to get by as cheaply as possible. A balance exists between cheap and too expensive. You can decide what is a good balance in your area.

Two final tips: (1) Allow people to enjoy themselves socially and educationally. (2) Give your singles a place to share their lives with other people, and educate them the best you know how. With a lavish application of these two principles, you cannot fail to grow as an increasingly effective group.

CLASS ORGANIZATION
AND LEADERSHIP

The final test of a leader is that he leaves behind him in other men the conviction and the will to carry on.
—*Walter Lippmann*, Roosevelt Has Gone

The most important questions you will answer for your ministry are: Who will lead? What type of leadership do we want? The who and what of your leadership will determine the future success of your singles ministry.

Churches have tried different methods of leadership in their efforts to develop a singles ministry. Each of these approaches fall into one of five types.

Let the Senior Minister Develop the Ministry

Many ordained ministers take upon themselves the job of developing a new singles ministry. Most of the time they prove unsuccessful. Why? Because they lack the time to devote to the ministry. Pastors fulfill so many duties, even in small churches, that they cannot spend enough quality time developing the singles ministry. A thriving singles ministry may require more than 100 person hours per week to maintain itself. The officers at very large churches spend more than 250 person hours per week. How can a pastor spend that much time on one ministry within his or her church?

Of course, the pastor can choose people to take care of the many tasks necessary to maintain the ministry. Still, he or she must make the key decisions for the ministry. What if the pastor chooses the wrong type of person to help with the program? I remember a pastor in an Arkansas church who chose a self-righteous man to lead the church's new singles ministry. He believed that all divorced people are particularly bad sinners. Singles will not tolerate this type of leadership. If they can find no other singles ministry to join, they will probably drop out of the church.

Another and even more serious problem exists if the senior pastor is in charge of the singles. The minister who started the ministry will support the ministry. If not, he would not have allowed the ministry to begin. But what if that pastor moves to another church and his or her replacement does not have the same goals for the ministry? What if the new minister does not believe in singles ministries? Not all ministers believe in separating singles from the rest of the congregation. More than one program has failed because of pastors moving to another church.

Hire a Singles Minister

This is not a possibility for many churches because of the expense of another salary. Even in larger churches that have the money to hire a singles minister, this option carries many of the same dangers as having the senior minister lead the ministry.

As I mentioned in an earlier chapter, your ministry must not be a one person show—which is what you can have if you hire a singles minister who does not thoroughly understand the importance of delegation. Many singles ministers choose the educational format, plan the parties, and organize the other activities of the singles ministry. What do the singles do? Merely show up when told to. They feel no responsibility to the ministry and will not get as involved as they should. The ministry is for them, not the singles minister. Singles need to look to one another for support and leadership, not a hired minister. A big emotional gap inevitably exists between an ordained minister and a layperson, especially single laypersons. Even when an ordained minister is single, he or she is still an ordained minister. Many singles ministry attendees will not feel comfortable at parties if he or she also attends. No matter how sincere a paid singles minister is about the ministry, the gap may stifle the ministry.

What if the singles minister should leave for another church? The next one may want to reorganize the ministry, which may not be all bad. The new one may decide to initiate new ideas. This is good. But what if he or she wants to completely change a growing ministry's format? The singles who felt comfortable with the ministry may not like the new format. You probably will lose some of your members who you must then replace.

Different singles ministers will have their own ideas about the educational format. What if a singles minister believes in teaching *only* the Bible? Most people believe the Bible is inspired, revealed, and the greatest book ever written. It does have the answers to many perplexing problems in our lives. But singles have a difficult time appreciating the relational problems of Samson and Delilah, to take one example. Singles need to learn about how to form a relationship. Singles need motivational books to help them learn how to rebuild their lives. Singles need to learn new social skills that the Bible cannot teach in a modern culture. Ministers who do not believe in teaching or reading any book or from any other discipline except the Bible—and then try to impart this view on a singles ministry—will probably experience disappointment when the ministry fails. They will wonder why, but still will not accept the fact that God's grace is available through many people and many other books.

Find a Married Couple to Sponsor the Class

Many churches have tried this method of leadership in their singles ministry. Married couples may have their heart in the right place, but they are not a part of the singles culture. *To be a leader of the people, you need to be of the people.* People who have never divorced cannot possibly understand the singles and their needs. Single people do understand and can help their peers. Married couples may make the singles feel worse about their lives. The married couple serve as a constant reminder of the divorced singles' collapsed marriages. When this happens, the ministry is having the opposite effect you want. Married couples do not, of course, mean for this to happen—but it happens.

If married, ask yourself a question: How would I like to walk into a singles-only Sunday school class? Would I feel comfortable? Ask yourself another question: Could they help me if I had marriage problems? The answer is yes, and they could and would help. They have been there. They know about marriage problems. The singles can help the married people with marriage problems. However, the married people cannot help the singles with most of their issues, because they are not experiencing the culture or the pain.

The term *sponsors* is a particularly difficult subject. Some churches extrapolate from I Timothy 5 and Paul's advice to a young pastor about the role of widows in the church. Apparently there were some problems with gossips. So it is presumed today, at least in some places, that these "tender, hurting persons" need "mature, married holy persons" to counsel against promiscuity and gossip. Singles ministries do not need sponsors who presume that the Great American Family is the only way to mature in faith and works. Many churches, therefore, make a deadly tactical mistake when they appoint married people as "sponsors" of the singles ministry. This is not a Scout troop for immature adults. Your singles are full-grown adults, not children, not failures, and not misfits. They are just persons whose marriages collapsed, or whose spouse died, or someone who is not married at this point in his or her life.

Remarried Couples Who Previously Have Been Single

If your church dogmatically insists on having someone other than the singles lead themselves, this is the best alternative. At least a remarried couple will understand the pain of divorce or widowhood and the trials of the singles culture, and what they must go through to rebuild their lives.

But one roadblock still exists—the leadership is married. They no longer belong in the singles culture. The couple, however, could be a model for those singles who want to remarry. But what if they experience marriage problems—and they may. Remarriages have their own set of problems. "What do we do about our separate property? Your kid gets more than mine. Do not discipline my child; I will do it. Your mother does not like me as much as she did your first wife (or husband)." The list of problems goes on and on. Singles are not usually ready to see this type of situation in the top leadership, though it is a reality. They must deal with their own set of life-changing issues first.

Let the Singles Develop the Ministry

If someone gives you something, will you feel less responsibility toward the item than if you had bought it yourself? How much better care will you give that object? Singles will feel the same way about their ministry if they retain the leadership. They need to experience and enjoy the thrill of watching their own creation grow. They need to feel the frustration any leader experiences when something he or she planned does not go perfectly. They need to feel the inner rewards when they watch a person grow because of an organization they helped create. They need to feel ownership of the ministry. After all, it is for their benefit.

81

A singles ministry that is led by the singles does not have any of the problems or disadvantages of the other four types of leadership. Though singles ministries have a rapid turnover, the leadership will always have a core group. This will give the ministry a continuity essential to any successful organization. Singles do not get paid for their efforts. They will get their paychecks in satisfaction for a job well done, one for which they were totally responsible.

Your ministry may not grow as fast, at first, as it might if a paid staff person or ordained minister is in charge. But your ministry will last longer. The old cliché is often true: It is not how you start that is important, but how you finish. It is especially true in singles organizations.

Many churches across America have tried the first four methods of leadership. These have usually proved unsuccessful, or not as successful as they could be. Churches that try to develop singles ministries do not need to try failed methods of leadership. Enough others have already done that. Let the singles lead, and your ministry will stand the test of time.

Officers and Their Duties

Select a core group of officers during the first week of your ministry. The organizational chart on the opposite page will give you an idea of how to choose them. Combine some offices if you do not have enough people to fill them. For example, you can combine the offices of party, recreation, and social until you get enough members to split them apart. As your ministry grows, each office will need a separate person to take charge. You can begin a ministry with as few as five officers: president, secretary, education, social, and newcomers. As your ministry grows, expand the number of offices as the need arises.

President

The president is responsible for the overall planning and motivation of the class and fellow officers. He or she

ORGANIZATION CHART FOR OFFICERS AND THEIR DUTIES

PRESIDENT

Overall planning & motivation, establish special task forces, spokesperson for class, conduct monthly meetings, coordinates with church minister

(Inside Activities)

TREASURER

Count attendance, collect offering, record receipts & payments, give report at board meetings, help care and concern

SECRETARY

Publish bulletin, keep minutes of meetings, class supplies, assist attendance, publish class directory

VICE-PRESIDENT

Plan and organize special events, (fund raising, spiritual retreats, service projects), fill in for president, organize & maintain class bulletin board and announcements

PARTY

Adult parties, dinners, dances, Christmas & New Year's events, reservations & arrangements

SOCIAL

Dinners for eight, Saturday Night live, holiday dinners

(Outside Activities)

RECREATION

Family-type activities, picnics, skating parties, movies, zoo trips, Sunday lunches

MUSIC

Plan and organize Sunday morning music, responsible for Picking 'N' Grinning

EDUCATION

Plan weekly program, plan room locations, serve on church committee for education

NEWCOMERS

Welcome visitors, hold Newcomers's class & parties, help newcomers become acquainted with class members

ATTENDANCE

Maintain class roster, compile names for class directory, keep changes of addresses

PUBLICITY

Publish monthly newsletter, maintain class phone recorder

SERVICE INVOLVEMENT

Develop ways for class to be involved with various community projects

CARE & CONCERN

Contact missing members, send cards / flowers to sick members / death in family, maintain class scrapbook establishes special committee/task-groups for special projects as selected by the board. The president will serve as general spokesperson for the ministry and conduct monthly board meetings. The president and the pastor should stay in touch. Your singles ministry should plan its activities so they do not conflict with the church's programs.

One word of caution: *The president should be someone who can and will delegate authority.* All the officers need the freedom to do their jobs as they see fit. If the president of the ministry tries to do the other officers' jobs, your ministry probably will not succeed. I had only two firm rules while president of a large group, and both worked well:

(1) *Each officer has total responsibility for his or her office and duties.* They fulfilled their duties as they saw fit. Unless they did something crazy, I supported their decisions 100 percent, despite the outcome. In three terms as president, I only had to step in and change a decision one time.

This rule allows each officer the chance to grow and learn on his or her own. Knowing he or she is in charge brings out the creativity and leadership in each. Your ministry will help people develop more talent than you ever thought possible. Give everyone the opportunity to grow and become more creative, and your ministry will grow and prosper.

(2) *Each officer is to stay in his own territory.* They are *never* to make a decision for another officer, regardless of the circumstances. If another officer interferes with the duties of someone else, serious dissension will develop among your officers. This will stifle your ministry's growth as nothing else. Each officer is a volunteer. They gladly give of their free time to help the class and want to take care of their office by themselves.

An example of what can happen if one officer interferes with another: Before I became president, I was party director. The social director and I had spent two months finding a place to hold Friday night socials. Each Friday we had about fifty to seventy-five people who attended. Not many restaurants can handle this type of crowd in addition to their regular patrons. She and I had located a major hotel that would welcome us for Friday night socials, if we agreed to hold our dances there. We made an agreement with the manager of the hotel on a Saturday. The next morning, during general assembly, the president informed the class he had agreed for our group to meet for Friday socials at another restaurant. Stunned is not the word for how the social director and I felt. Two months of hard work was wasted. The president would not change his mind when we told him about our arrangement with the hotel. Our class did not have bylaws at the time, and we could not make him change his mind. The major hotel did not appreciate our backing out, not one little bit. The social director and I got mad at the president, and he got angry with us. Do not let this happen in your ministry. Volunteer jobs do not pay money. Singles have enough to do to maintain themselves and their life-style. They do not need to spend their time working for the ministry, only to see their plans reversed, unless they make a decision that will harm the ministry.

Another important duty of the president is to be a public relations person for the ministry. As the class grows, this will become even more necessary. He or she should attend all the social functions, if possible.

Vice-president

The vice-president plans and organizes special events. These include fundraising, retreats, and special service projects. He or she will maintain a bulletin board with notices that inform the class of special trips, retreats, property rentals, or job opportunities.

The primary responsibility of the vice-president is to help the president with his or her duties. Occasionally, the president will need to miss a Sunday morning or a board meeting. The vice-president should possess the leadership skills to take over the responsibilities of leading the class. The group should select the vice-president as carefully as they do the president. Most singles ministries experience a high rate of turn-over in membership. If the president should get married, move, or otherwise resign, the vice-president will step up to the office of president.

The president and the vice-president need to know that they can work together. Problems will arise in the class, and the president needs someone he or she can turn to for advice. Your board of officers cannot meet every time the president needs advice. If the president has a vice-president to help make a decision, the class will run smoother.

Secretary

The secretary will prepare and publish a weekly class bulletin and a monthly calendar of events. He or she will take and maintain minutes of the class board meetings. The secretary's responsibilities also include obtaining the necessary supplies such as pens, pencils, name tags, and any other supplies necessary for the class to function.

The secretary distributes a bulletin every Sunday morning. Include the week's calendar of events, the classes offered that day, and future events. Also, mail a copy of this to newcomers and prospective members. The bulletin does not need to be fancy. One page will suffice until you have enough information to enlarge it.

The monthly calendar outlines the events of each month. You need to make enough copies so all members and guests can have one. Newcomers will want one and some members will misplace theirs. Mailing out the calendar and bulletin will encourage any prospective members to participate in class activities.

Treasurer

The treasurer collects the offerings (many ministries give one-half of their offerings to the church). The treasurer maintains a record of receipts and payments for the class and makes reports at the class board meetings. He or she also maintains a bank account for the class. Most organizations require two signatures for each check written. The president, vice-president, secretary, or treasurer can sign checks. Any two can sign the checks.

If you do not have enough members, combine the secretary and treasurer. Once your ministry becomes large enough, you will need to split the offices.

Social Director

Dinners for Eight, and Saturday Night Live are the responsibilities of this director. Specific duties will be discussed in the activities chapter. Holiday dinner planning is also in the job description of the social director. Singles without family members nearby need somewhere to go for special holidays such as Thanksgiving, July 4th, Easter, and Christmas. Did you ever have to spend one of these holidays alone? Ask for volunteers to use their home for the dinner. Then, plan a budget and a menu with the host, who does not spend any money on the dinner. Their contribution is their home. The host should call the people who plan to attend and find out what they want to bring.

For Christmas and Thanksgiving, do not have a potluck dinner. We all think of certain traditional menus for these two holidays. The holiday seasons will magnify the hurt of a person newly singled. Not spending time with your family is heart-rending when everyone else is with theirs. The people who come to these dinners will love you for your efforts.

Recreation Director

The recreation director plans and coordinates all class family-type activities. These include picnics, skating parties, movies, zoo trips, and camping. Recreation also plans Sunday lunch locations. He or she should inform the secretary as soon as possible, so the dates and places can be put into the bulletin.

Party Director

The party director plans and coordinates all adult parties, dinners, and dances. His or her duties include making reservations at any place the class will use. Also, he or she needs to make available decorations and supplies for the parties. Party and social directors will work together on certain events. The activities chapter will explain more about this.

Care and Concern Director

Many singles live alone. When sick, they will appreciate a phone call, flowers, or a personal visit. The care and concern director is responsible for this duty. In more cases than you might think, this may be the only contact some singles have while sick, in the hospital, or in some other crisis. Many singles may not have family members living close enough to help them in an emergency. Nothing is worse than lying in a hospital room by yourself and not having any visitors.

The class treasurer pays the bills for flowers and cards. The class needs to set up an account with a flower shop. Sometimes, the care and concern director will need a check from the treasurer, and he or she is unavailable. By opening an account, the director can pick up the phone and send flowers without delay. Most flower shops will send the class a monthly bill. The Board of Directors should establish guidelines for sending flowers to members in the hospital or at the death of a loved one.

Music Director

The main responsibility of the music director is to take charge of the music on Sunday morning. He or she is also responsible for Pickin' 'N' Grinnin'. This social event is discussed more thoroughly in the activities chapter.

He or she may wish to start an all-singles choir to go Christmas caroling and do special programs for the church. Organizing your own choir will give the singles ministry more visibility in the church. As the church members watch your program grow, and see the singles contribute their time and money to the church and community, they will become much more accepting of the ministry.

Attendance Registrar

This officer will take roll and count attendance on Sunday morning. He or she also will keep addresses and compile a class directory. Most singles ministries will experience a 90 percent turn-over about every six months. A new directory needs to be published every six months.

As your ministry grows, the directory will become more expensive to produce. You can ask the self-employed members to put a small advertisement in the directory. Charge $10 for a business-card-size advertisement. Establishments you frequent for outside social activities probably will place a small advertisement with you. The advertisements will help offset the cost of the directory if it is large. Remember, a singles ministry *can* financially sustain itself.

A word of caution: The class members will know the attendance registrar has a list of the names, addresses, and phone numbers of the class. He or she will get calls from members asking for the phone numbers and addresses of members of the opposite sex. The director needs to use caution in supplying information to someone he or she does not know. If the director gives out the information about someone, and trouble is caused, serious legal problems may occur.

Newcomer Director

This person welcomes visitors, signs them in, and introduces them to other members of the class. The director is responsible for arranging a Newcomer party once a month. The purpose of the party is to help new people get acquainted with one another and the regular members. The party also helps the newcomers begin to participate in class activities. Learning new social skills is never easy after a divorce or the death of a spouse. Newly singled people can learn these skills in the nonthreatening situations provided by class social events.

The newcomer director holds a class each Sunday morning

to answer questions the newcomers might ask about the class. As your ministry grows, you might develop a slide show to show the various activities of the class. Another method is to videotape the events and show them on a VCR. This will help familiarize the newcomers with all the events the class provides for them. Keep the newcomers together as a class for two weeks. The first week they go to a class called Newcomers I. Tell them about the class educational curricula and the social functions. The second week they go to Newcomers II. If you are in a larger congregation, you might give them a tour of the church and explain the various church functions. You might also have each newcomer tell what their hobbies are, how many children they have, and where they work. The third week, this group will become members of the class and can go to the class of their chioce. This integration process will allow them to get acquainted with a smaller number of people. As your ministry grows, this will become even more important. Imagine walking into a room with a hundred or more people standing around talking. If you have recently experienced divorce or the loss of a spouse and have not yet dealt with your pain, your self-esteem is not at an all-time high. Having to meet new people may be more than you can handle.

The newcomer director needs to be an extrovert, maybe more so than any other officer. He or she probably is the first contact the newcomers will have with your singles ministry. If you do not greet the visitors and make them feel welcome, they may not come back. People newly divorced or widowed will feel nervous about visiting your ministry. Most will not have yet gained back their self-esteem and may come to the class with a defensive attitude. A friendly face at the door will do wonders to reassure them that help is available.

The first Sunday they visit, the newcomers wear a yellow name tag. The second Sunday they wear a pink one, and the third Sunday they wear a blue name tag. This helps the regular class members to identify the newcomers. The fourth Sunday they wear an orange nametag and become a member of the class.

CLASS ORGANIZATION AND LEADERSHIP

Education Director

The education director plans and coordinates weekly lesson programs and arranges for facilitators, teachers, and guest speakers. He or she prepares and maintains a roster of lesson plans and room locations of the scheduled classes.

Singles require different educational material than other types of Sunday school classes. Most of your members will have divorced and be in the process of rebuilding their lives. Therefore, your class must feature more than Bible study. This does not mean you should not use the Bible and teach God's word. You must, however, base many of your classes on self-improvement or "recovery" books, ones that will help the singles rebuild their lives. You can teach these books with Christian presuppositions. Many ministries have successfully used the bibliography located after the last chapter to choose study books. In the late 1980s and early 1990s, these books have become very popular and are readily available in many bookstores.

Some churches require Sunday school classes to use their own denominational quarterlies or subject material. If forced to do this, your singles ministry may falter if some material is not designed with the singles culture in mind. As stated earlier, singles may feel anger toward God. They need to restore their faith in themselves and in God. Until they can come to terms with themselves, they will have a difficult time doing so. The now-familiar list of stressful life events places divorce second, after the death of a spouse. People must go through the grief process before they can start to rebuild their lives. Self-help books facilitate progress through the grief process and help singles begin a new life.

New ministries may not have enough members to offer different classes on Sunday morning. Until then, pick a self-improvement book and teach from it. As the class grows, more people will offer to teach. People dealing with a specific problem, such as relationships, will make effective teachers.

An excellent method of teaching in a singles ministry is to combine lecture and class discussion. Singles need to verbalize how they feel about many topics; talking will help them to heal. They can express anger, sadness, and the other emotions that go with divorce or widowhood. Other members of the class can lend them a sympathetic ear and offer suggestions on how to cope with their grief. This is another strong advantage of a singles ministry. Married people will have a difficult time relating to a single's pain.

A close friend is about twenty years older. One morning he and I started a lively discussion about being young and old. He made a statement that stopped the discussion, cold. He said, "Harry, I can tell you a whole lot about being young, but you can't tell me one thing about being old." End of discussion. Married people can tell singles a lot about staying married. But they cannot empathize with what people experience when they divorce or become widowed. Sympathize, they might, but a difference exists in the experiences and thinking of the two cultures.

Another type of class that will prove successful is "open discussion." Any topic the group wants to discuss is the format. The facilitator needs to direct and focus the discussion—a skill that comes only through experience. A class of this type is comparable to a group therapy session. Open discussion will give the hurting singles in your group a place to vent their feelings and come to terms with themselves. But an open discussion also has some dangers. It can easily go astray. If the facilitator is not careful, the topic will go in the direction of the greatest pain. This direction is not inherently bad, provided that most members of the group are in the same place in their lives. But what if several class members have already dealt with their pain in the area where the discussion leads? If the teacher permits the class to get hung up on one subject, only a small minority will benefit.

Many singles ministries tend to deal only with pain, and this is not a healthy sign. Many of your members will have already dealt with the pain of their loss, whether divorced or widowed. You need to offer uplifting classes for them—using topics that will help them improve their lives. If most of the classes deal with pain, you will find it harder to attract new members who have dealt with theirs. People who are now past their traumas will serve as a lighthouse for the hurting, but those who have recovered need good class sessions too. Find a balance; otherwise your ministry will not grow.

A Wednesday night study group can be a popular segment of education for your ministry. People will feel more relaxed in an informal setting such as this. You can hold a mid-week meeting at the church, in someone's home, or at an apartment clubhouse. Most singles look forward to being around friends in the middle of the week. Your imagination is the only boundary for the topics. You may want to talk on subjects such as how to develop a successful relationship, coping with loneliness, and single-parenting problems. The mid-week meeting needs to uplift the feelings of the participants. No one wants to go to a meeting and leave with a feeling of depression.

The education director has an important job in a singles ministry, if not the most important. A good mixture of classes, including Bible study and self-improvement studies, will help your members look forward to coming to Sunday school. Your most popular topics will revolve around relationships. The members of any singles ministry have experienced problems with relationships. If they did not, they would not want to become a member of your singles ministry. They will be eager to better learn how to get along with the opposite sex than they have in the past. A major part of this will involve learning how to love themselves. In return, their relationship with God will improve, resulting in a stronger human being.

Once your ministry has enough members, you might want to teach a special class for those just out of a divorce or recently widowed. An excellent book to teach in this class is *Rebuilding When Your Relationship Ends* by Bruce Fisher. The main topic is the grief process and how to move through the fifteen steps to overcoming grief. Most people do not understand the grief process. Once they do, any time they suffer a loss, they can deal with the pain more skillfully.

Service Involvement Director

This director organizes ways for the class members to become involved in providing help and service to the community. Organizations such as Big Brothers and Big Sisters, the Red Cross, Salvation Army, and the United Way always need volunteers. Your church also will have outreach and service activities in which the singles can help.

The service and involvement is a difficult but rewarding job. Singles whose children live with them may enjoy little free time for volunteer work. However, many singles live alone and will enjoy helping other people. Saturdays and Sundays can be long and lonesome when a person first divorces or becomes a widow. Community work is an excellent way for them to get back into the mainstream of life.

Publicity Director

The publicity director prepares and publishes a monthly newspaper. You may never feel the need for this type of service to your ministry, but many ministries do send out a newsletter. You can include articles on single living, the upcoming activities, and other news items about the members of the class. The newsletter will be good publicity for your ministry.

This director also records weekly activities on the class telephone message machine. Many ministries install a telephone recorder to announce the next week's events. You can buy one that reports for about $50 to $60. The recorder will require a separate telephone line at commercial rates, costing about $35 per month. If you don't want to go to the expense of the extra telephone line, find a member who will volunteer to put the player at his or her home.

Class Membership

Visitors might become members after attending three times. After the third Sunday, place their names on the mailing list and the membership roster. You might consider taking the time to record emergency information about your new members. Many singles live alone and their families may live far away. In case a class member becomes hospitalized and unable to communicate with his or her family, who do you contact?

At a Lake Day, one of our members had a serious motorcycle accident. He needed immediate brain surgery, and we did not know how to contact his family or his children. Fortunately, his ex-wife still had her telephone listed in his name. She helped us contact his children and parents. His accident made us take action. We now keep a file with enough information to help find a person's family. Keep the file at the church. You never know when you will need it. If an officer keeps the information at his or her home, it might not be available when needed.

Age Grouping

Many ministries separate their groups by ages. I do not recommend that you do this. Young people need the wisdom and the experience of the older members. The older members need the youthful enthusiasm of the young. Each can learn from the other. The secular singles culture does not separate people by age. Why do so in a singles ministry?

It is also very difficult to group singles by age. Some younger singles will want to mingle with the older members. A few members will get caught in the middle and not fit into either age group. This may cause them not to join the ministry. People need to feel a sense of belonging in Sunday school. Let the members decide who they want to associate with.

When I first heard about a singles ministry, I went to visit. The church had separated the ministry into two age groups—one for ages thirty to fifty, and the other for those over fifty. The over-fifty class averaged closer to age sixty. The people in the thirty to fifty class had an average age of less than thirty. I was forty and did not fit into either group.

Uncomfortable with either one, I did not join that church's singles ministry. A mixed group of all ages will give everyone the option of mingling with people with whom they feel comfortable, regardless of age.

On the other hand, if you live in a large city and your ministry attains several hundred members, you may want to make an exception to age grouping. The early twenties may want to form their own class. Their life-style is different from someone in their forties or fifties. They enjoy a different type of music, are still in a transient place in life, and will have different ideas about life. They also will require a different type of educational format. Most of them will not have divorced and will not relate to the rest of the class.

Integration into the Church

Many people who join the singles ministry also will join the church. Many will not, so do not expect everyone to become a member of your church. Part of your group will come to class on Sunday and then go to their home church for services. Some of these split-level attendees do this because of their children's involvement in the other church. Also, their home church may not have a singles ministry. Do not forget that your primary purpose in forming a singles ministry is to help people find their way in a new and strange world. Your church will serve as a beacon in the night to lonely people who feel stranded in a dark time in their lives. But not all of these people will decide to join your particular society.

Remember, too, that many singles who attend Sunday classes will come from another denomination. A singles ministry in a United Methodist church, for example, may have Baptists, Catholics, Jews, and many other denominations represented. For some Christians, this pluralism spells trouble, but it is a characteristic of any growing singles ministry. Singles will attend and grow by learning from one another. Surely God does not judge us if we share our common beliefs and talk about those matters of faith where we differ.

The singles who do join your church will become dedicated and excellent members. You can integrate many of them into your regular church committees. Two out of the last three chairmen of the Administrative Board of my church were past presidents of our singles ministry. We were single when we held the top leadership position in the church. Many skills that the singles learn while leading the ministry will benefit the church committees.

The larger your ministry becomes, the more teachers and leaders you will obtain for the rest of the church. These singles do not lack the talent or skills to become dedicated church leaders. A few church leaders still have strange thoughts about singles because of the "divorced" stigma. This attitude is changing. Many people know a minister who has divorced, which does not make that person different—just no longer married. The ability to preach is not impaired. The skill at leading the church is not altered.

Mixing married people and singles on church committees will help the married people to understand better the singles and their life-style. Though a person may have enjoyed a thirty year marriage, the chances are almost 100 percent that someone in his or her family has divorced. Working side by side with a single will help married persons become more accepting and understanding of singles.

—— IV ——
ACTIVITIES

The family is the association established by nature for the supply of man's everyday wants.

—Aristotle

Successful singles ministries require an active social calendar. Singles want and need to spend time with their peers. Many of your members will have no families to visit at night or on the weekends. Erich Fromm's concept applies here—people need to be a part of one another, and to be around their peers. An active social schedule fills that need and will make your program more successful.

Social activities also will serve another important purpose. Members of your class may have been married for twenty or twenty-five years or longer. They may have forgotten how to make acquaintances with the opposite sex. They will have forgotten the etiquette of dating. They may not know about the new dating rules. They may not know that women do ask men for dates and pay for them. They may not know how to form Platonic friendships with the opposite sex.

The activities listed below are group oriented. Singles will learn how to get to know one another in a safe situation. Men and women can learn how to ease back into society. They can get to know their peers in a safe situation before they start dating. Remember, a vast gulf exists between married and single cultures. Your ministry will teach the singles new social skills.

As the membership of your ministry grows, the social calendar should expand. However, do not schedule every night until your ministry has grown to 100 members or more. If you try to schedule too much at first the events may not be well attended. As your ministry grows, you will have enough members to make each activity well attended. Different people will enjoy different activities. Some will enjoy going to movies, others may prefer to go on a nature walk, and some would like to have small sing-alongs.

Weekend activities will be the most important for your ministry. For single people, these times can be long and lonesome. Parents who do not have their children with them during what we consider family time may feel at wits' end. Offer them an opportunity to spend time with their friends. Many ministries have successfully used the activities listed in this chapter. Some of these may not be possible in your area, but the list will give you some ideas about where to start. Members of your class will contribute other excellent suggestions.

Sunday Lunch

Many members of your class will enjoy Sunday lunch. After all, gathering the family for a lunch of fried chicken, gravy, potatoes, and apple pie is an American tradition. Eating by yourself after church on Sunday can be depressing. Sunday afternoon is probably the worst time of the week for people recently singled. Sunday is family day in America, but their family no longer exists. Where do they go? Who can they spend their time with?

The recreation director is in charge of finding reasonably priced restaurants for Sunday lunch. Most singles have limited budgets. Your members will enjoy hamburger places, Mexican, Chinese, and pizza restaurants. The more expensive the menu, the fewer the people who can afford to join you for lunch. Rotate restaurants if possible. This gives everyone a chance to eat their favorite meal. The important point for Sunday lunch is not to have a gourmet meal but to socialize. The recreation director might also plan for the group to go to a movie, play softball, or visit the zoo.

Friday Night Fellowship

Friday Night Fellowship is a popular event with most ministries. Busy with their jobs during the week, people may not have seen each other. They will look forward to spending time with friends at the end of the week. Hold this activity at someone's home, or anywhere people can mingle and visit. Your best place to go is a public establishment. Restaurants, if you call in advance, can set aside a special room for you.

One ministry has their primary weekly activity on Friday evening. They meet at the church about 6:30 P.M. and have a potluck dinner. Then, they have an educational program led by a member of the group. About 10:00 P.M., they adjourn and go to a local coffee house and talk. Your group can decide what type of Friday evenings it wants.

Saturday Mornings

Some of your members will enjoy scheduled outdoor activities on Saturday morning. Those who want to can ride bikes, go to the lake, play tennis, or whatever is fun to do in your area. Singles have to do all the house cleaning, grocery shopping, washing, and ironing by themselves. They may have to spend their Saturdays taking care of chores. Check with the group. They will let you know their desires.

Breakfasts for Eight

This will be one of your more popular activities. People arise early and meet at someone's home for breakfast. A month before the scheduled breakfast, the social director puts out a sign-up sheet. This form has a place for hosts and hostesses to volunteer to have the breakfast in their homes. The host or hostess selects the menu. He or she then calls the people assigned to their home and informs each guest of what to bring. The host or hostess provides only the place for the breakfast. The social director divides the people who sign up into equal groups, with men and women assigned as evenly as possible. In a large city, consider dividing breakfast groups into zip codes. This keeps people from having to travel an hour to eat breakfast.

After the breakfast, the recreation director may want to plan a day at the lake, skiing, or hiking to finish off the day. Each geographical area will have some fun activities to do that will differ from other parts of the country. After-breakfast activities are not necessary, but your members will enjoy the day and, of course, it provides more opportunities for community building.

Saturday Night Live

Schedule these once a month. Hold this small party at someone's home or apartment. You can have a cook-out, potluck, or just have everyone bring something to share. The purpose of Saturday Night Live is to provide those without dates somewhere to go. When a person is single, spending Saturday evening alone can be depressing. People will enjoy playing games, talking, or just relaxing. As in all the social activities, fellowship is the key.

Newcomer Parties

A couple of months into your singles program, start scheduling Newcomer Parties. No other activity will help your ministry grow more than this one. Newcomers will enjoy meeting new people somewhere other than the church. You can have this on a Saturday night, a Thursday night, or any night the board of directors believes is appropriate. A week-night party has the disadvantage of having to break up early. Because they go to work the next morning, people must go home earlier than they might want. A Friday or Saturday night is probably your best choice. Once you choose a night to have the party, stay with it. Do not change unless you have a valid purpose.

A Newcomer's Party will help new people get to know regular class members. Ideally, hold this party at someone's home or apartment. This is a casual, relaxed setting, and the people will enjoy the homey atmosphere.

Your Newcomer Parties will have better attendance if you send out invitations to the newcomers who attended Sunday mornings during the previous month. This is another reason to keep their names and addresses. The invitations do not need to be fancy. All you want to do is inform them where and when the party will be held.

Pickin' 'n' Grinnin'

The music director is in charge of this social that is held at someone's home or apartment. Pickin' n' Grinnin' is similar to Saturday Night Live, except that it is a sing-along. People can bring their guitars, harmonicas, or bongo drums and have a fun, relaxed evening. The hosts may ask that everyone bring a snack to share. Another option is for the class to budget enough money so the host can provide some snacks and something to drink. Any time someone offers his or her home for a social event, either the individual members or the class pays the expenses.

Movie and Pizza Night

Meet at the church, go to your favorite pizza place, and then to a movie of your choice. An event such as this will help people adjust to being single. You can call this type of event a group-dating situation. People get to know one another, relax, and have others with whom to share their lives. This is a nonthreatening social event. Women will feel comfortable on a Movie and Pizza Night. There really is safety in numbers.

Dinners for Eight

This probably will be the most popular social activity of your ministry. This event is another excellent way for members to get to know one another in a relaxed setting. Breakfasts for Eight and Dinners for Eight have the same format. Breaking bread with someone helps to remove social barriers and provides an excellent atmosphere for making new friends. Newly singled people will feel safe in a home. They can start to learn how to participate in the single's culture.

The social director provides sign-up sheets a month in advance. Encourage the class members to sign up each week. The week before the dinners, divide the names into groups of eight. Give the lists of the people and their phone numbers to the hosts and hostesses, whose main duty is to provide the place for the dinner. They select the menu and help the guests to decide what they want to bring. Choices can range from the main dish to desserts, rolls, and napkins. Some men like to cook and some women prefer rolls or the beverage.

The social director should try to divide the men and women as evenly as possible. No one wants to go to a dinner with all people of the same sex. Your dinners will be much better attended and enjoyed more if you can have an equal numbers of men and women attend each. As in all singles groups, however, the membership will have more women than men. You will just have to do the best you can with what you have.

Another variation on Breakfasts for Eight and Dinners for Eight is to have a progressive menu. The social director will have more work to do, but this will add some spice to your socials.

Each host or hostess provides a different part of the meal. The class members meet, for example, at the first house for salad. Then they car-pool to the next house for vegetables. At the next home, they have the main course, and the final stop will be for dessert. One rule is that a passenger must not ride in the same car twice. This allows people to become better acquainted with more class members. The same system will work for progressive Breakfasts for Eight. If your class has more than fifty members, the logistics of a progressive meal will swamp even the most organized of social directors.

Whatever variations you use, ask the hosts not to tell the people assigned to their home who will be there. Instead, tell them they will be pleasantly surprised. If you tell people in advance and they do not know everyone or do not care for those attending, they may decide not to attend. This is not a pleasant trait among singles, but it is reality. Dinners are better attended if you do not give out the guest list beforehand.

Schedule the dinner for around 6:30 to 7:00 P.M. An after dinner party is an excellent time for the smaller groups to come together as one large group. People will have full tummies, be laughing, and be in good spirits. They will have spent the evening meeting new people and will continue that process at the large gathering.

If your denomination permits, an after-dinner dance is fun. Hold this at an apartment clubhouse, a motel ballroom, or even at the church. The party director makes the arrangements. Some ministries gather as a large group and serve coffee and dessert. The main goal is to bring the large group under one roof so they can get to know one another better.

You probably think that singles stay busy, and you are right. They constantly stay on the move and look for people to be with. The social activities will help them comfortably merge into the singles culture. After all, many people were married for years. Relearning social skills can prove difficult for both men and women.

Providing suitable and enjoyable social activities is another good reason for having a singles ministry. They will find a place to spend their time around people. Your goal is to provide a place where this can happen in a safe and comfortable setting. Singles want more substantial friendships and activities than they can find in the so-called "bar scene."

Fund Raising

A properly structured and organized ministry will provide its own funding. Once you begin to draw large numbers of people to your ministry, you will need cash for operating expenses. You will need deposits for parties and money for office and classroon supplies. The ministry may be encouraged to help other causes, such as the missions programs at the church.

A "Slave Auction" is an excellent source of income. Make this an annual event and hold it on a Saturday night in the early spring or fall. Having an auction before a new set of officers takes office does them a real favor. They will start with some money in the bank to take care of the financial needs of your ministry.

The vice-president provides a sign-up sheet about a month before the auction. People can donate different skills or talents that will go to the highest bidder. An interior designer can volunteer free consultation. A carpenter can donate time to do some repair work. A mechanic can give a free tune-up. People can offer sailboat rides, a night out on the town, a home-cooked meal, house cleaning, or anything else that a person can provide for another person. One popular item that always brings a good price: A person who will give a candlelight dinner for someone. The list of items to sell is endless and your imagination is your only boundary.

The buyer and the seller need to sign a contract. This way, everyone understands his or her obligation. Not fulfilling an agreement in a church affair is not a penitentiary offense, but it can cause hard feelings. People who donate money for the class deserve to receive the service they bought. You will find a sample contract in the Special Forms section.

Some members of your class may feel reluctant to donate a service to the auction. A primary reason for this may be their lack of self-esteem. People may tell you something different, but this probably will be the reason. They may fear that no one will buy their service. I have never seen this happen at any of our auctions. Everything is always purchased by someone. Encourage them a little. Tell them that they will help the class to help others. Knowing they will help the ministry to raise money will encourage them to participate.

The class also can work together to have garage sales. When you combine several people's items, you can raise some more money. In addition, working together in this way provides still another opportunity for fellowship and for making friends.

Retreats

A weekend retreat can be a sharing and caring time for class members. These can serve as times of spiritual renewal and growth, important for people recently divorced or widowed. A retreat can have various themes, such as working on self-esteem, goal-setting, and single-parenting. We have two retreats a year at our denomination's encampment. If you do not have a similar facility available, you can hold a retreat at a park near a lake or any other appropriate place.

Retreats begin on Friday nights. We arrive at the camp in time for a potluck dinner. This gives us a chance to get to know one another before the actual planned programs begin. We sit around the fireplace, talk, and do a preview of the structured part of the retreat. We schedule the structured part of the retreat for Saturday and Sunday. Schedule some free time so people can go for a nature walk, take a short nap, or do some more visiting with their new-found friends.

The vice-president takes care of the retreats, each of which needs to revolve around a special educational theme. My denomination sponsors a retreat on "Human Sexuality." This may be a helpful topic for your ministry. Members of the class, counselors, or other professionals can speak on other special topics.

ACTIVITIES

Divorce Adjustment Workshop

The Divorce Adjustment Workshop is a major attraction for singles ministry members and perhaps the most important ministry for any group. The workshop is designed for newly divorced singles or those ending a significant relationship. The workshop is not only a means of attracting new members for your class, but it also fills a definite need within the community. About 80 percent of singles ministry members join because of a Divorce Adjustment Workshop.

People hurting from the pains of divorce need somewhere to go and heal. These workshops are popular, well attended, self-sustaining, and will be the primary source of your growth. The church's growth will benefit as much as your singles ministry. The more members your singles ministry has, the more new members your church will have. About nine thousand people have participated in Phoenix's workshops. We now conduct eight of these workshops each year, with each having between forty and sixty participants. You cannot imagine how fulfilled your leaders will feel after they have conducted a Divorce Adjustment Workshop. They will have helped some of their peers get over the trauma of one of the most painful experiences that adults have to endure. A DA workshop is a caring, sharing, and repairing experience that will broaden your ministry as nothing else can.

An effective workshop must have structure. The members of the ministry staff the workshop. Phoenix has developed its own structure over the last ten years. You will need twenty persons on the staff to have a workshop. The leadership teams include a course facilitator, enabler observers, small group facilitators, and a care team."

Your church might consider two types of Divorce Adjustment Workshops. One, a week-end workshop, starts Friday evening and runs until Sunday night. Participants go home at night and come back the next morning. The other might be called a LEO Workshop, an acronym for Life Enrichment Opportunities. Several of these workshops can be held each year. The divorce seminar is one of the classes offered during the workshop. The LEO workshops, held on successive Sunday nights, last for five weeks. The format is the same for both types.

The DA workshop format includes lecture and small group activities, with special emphasis on the small groups. This allows people to share their pain with people sympathetic to their plight, people who have experienced divorce. Topics discussed in the workshop are the grief process and how to use it to rebuild your life, common elements men and women have in a divorce, how to rebuild your self-esteem, finding happiness in the singles culture, where to turn when needing help, how to trust again, and how to avoid feeling guilty.

The small group discussions are invaluable for the participants. A man and a woman, who have been through the workshop, facilitate the small group discussion. Their purpose is to give the small group people a chance to talk, to cry, to laugh, or anything else that will help them put their divorce in the past. A facilitator's duty is not to advise, but to listen. He or she also needs to see that everyone gets a chance to talk.

The Course Facilitator is in charge of the workshop. The next level of leadership is called enabler observers, called EOs for short. They watch over the small group activity to ensure that the small group facilitators keep the group moving smoothly. If a small group facilitator needs any supplies—such as Kleenex, pencils, or paper—the EOs obtain them. This allows the facilitators to concentrate on their group.

A DA workshop also needs what we call a care team. This is a group of four or five people in charge of providing refreshments for the staff at breaks. They also take care of obtaining supplies when the EOs need them. You can charge $10 to $15 to pay for the refreshments and the supplies you need for the workshop. The participants who can afford to pay will do so. If someone does not have the necessary money, give them a scholarship. Do not turn anyone down because of lack of money on their part.

To serve on the leadership team, a person starts as a care

team member. Then, they can become a small group facilitator. After that they become EOs, giving them the experience necessary to lead a workshop. To serve on the staff, a person must have been a participant in the DA workshop. No one can know the entire process until they fill all the steps in the workshop. A small group facilitator, having been a participant, can understand how someone feels baring their soul to a small group. The most important thing is that they will learn even more about how to cope with their own divorce.

A Divorce Adjustment Workshop should not be facilitated by professional counselors. The purpose of the professional is to give special talks on the divorce process, self-esteem, or any other number of topics. The best facilitator is someone not too far removed from their own divorce. They will feel a sensitivity for the participant that the professional cannot. The secret to the DA workshop's success is that all members of the staff have suffered through the pain of divorce or the ending of a significant relationship.

You may have some participants seriously considering suicide. By the end of the workshop, they will probably be laughing and have some hope for their lives. Occasionally, you will have someone come to the workshop who will need professional help, and immediately. Always have someone on standby who can professionally counsel that person. We have had several participants who were in dangerous depression and did eventually commit suicide, which can devastate some groups to the point of collapse.

Once you have several workshops behind you, start mixing your experienced small group facilitators with inexperienced ones. This will always give you enough experienced facilitators to hold workshops. Singles groups have a rapid turnover. If you do not always have people in training, you may find yourself with not enough facilitators. Never let this happen. The workshop is a vital service to your ministry and to the community. The Divorce Adjustment Workshop will become the most important segment of your ministry.

THE VITAL SINGLES MINISTRY

Living as a Single

This workshop is for those who have recovered from divorce. Here, people will find a place to reshape their lives and set new goals. Speakers address such topics as careers, relationship skills, goal setting, single-parenting, and step-parenting.

The Divorce Adjustment Workshop and the Singles Living Workshop provide for different needs. Offer both and you will cover the needs of not only the newly divorced but the long-time singles as well. This will give you a balanced singles ministry.

To be successful, concentrate on the needs of all singles, not just the newly divorced. If you structure your ministry on divorce needs only, you will not have a healthy program. You will have too much pain. People in pain need to see and spend time around others who have outgrown their own pain and have put their lives together again.

Elections

If you follow the guidelines in this book, there will come a time when you have enough members to hold elections. In the beginning of your ministry, people may have to volunteer for positions because the class does not have enough members to hold elections. You will, however, eventually have enough members to have elections.

People will work harder and do a better job if they volunteer to run and then win the office. Those who run against the winners will make excellent assistants. The assistants will get valuable experience and can step up at the next election to the main officer's job. You will find a nomination form in the Special Forms chapter. Try to avoid having people nominated who have no knowledge that they are about to run for office.

Our church has a rule that an officer must also be a member of the church. That way, people running for office will feel more a part of the inner workings of the church. They will do their job with the best interests of the church in mind. At first, you may not have enough officers in your group to enforce this, but you need to do so when possible.

Your officers need to serve no longer than six months, long enough for singles. Any less and the officers will hardly get started until their term runs out. Any longer and they will get tired. Phoenix had always used a six-month term of office, until I started my third term. Past leaders and I discussed changing the terms to a year. This seemed like a long time to serve a group as large as Phoenix. We compromised and changed the terms to nine months. However, the longer term did not work out. When we left office, most of the officers had burned out.

Nine months may not seem like a long time, but as you grow you will begin to understand. A six-month term keeps the officers excited and full of enthusiasm. They begin to understand their job around the end of the second month. The next two or three months will be the most productive time of their term. The last month or two, they are ready to step down and let someone else take over.

Elections might be held the second Sunday in March and the second Sunday in September. The new officers would take office the first Sunday in April and the first Sunday in October. Any six-month spread that suits you is okay. You may decide to begin new offices in January and July. One advantage to April and October is that most ministries plan no large activities for those months. Inexperienced officers do not need to start their terms with a large activity. They will need a few weeks to get the feel of their office.

After you have enough members in your program, appoint a Nominating Committee two months before the actual election. Perhaps choose five members of the class to serve on the committee, two board members and three members of the class. You need to have two of one sex and three of the other. This keeps the election committee as fair as possible.

You might think this is too structured for a Sunday school class. However, the singles ministry will grow into a large class before you know it, and politics are a part of large groups. You will find the rules for elections in the Bylaws.

Elections can be fun. Candidates have given parties, furnished election T-shirts, and created some different campaigns. This probably will not happen for the first year or two, but elections will add some bonding to your ministry.

Toastmasters

The larger your ministry gets, the better trained and efficient your officers must become. Teachers must have the skills to present excellent lessons on Sunday. You will need trained leaders for your workshops and retreats. Most people never receive any leadership training or learn how to speak effectively.

Toastmasters is an excellent training method to teach leadership and the ability to speak. The larger your ministry becomes, the more qualified teachers and leaders you will need. The time will come when you can start your own Toastmasters Club. Toastmasters will not only prepare your members for your ministry, but also will help them advance in their personal careers.

As you can see from the list of events, not all are fun socials. Some will help your members overcome the pain of their divorce, while others will help the singles learn how to live in their new culture. Still, others will be strictly fun events. A successful ministry needs to have a balance of all three. As your ministry grows, you can add the activities as necessary. When you get large enough to have the workshops and the various activities, you will need about fifty members. You will need Divorce Adjustment and Single Living facilitators and leaders, officers, and teachers. The core group will be responsible for a smooth running organization. This is another reason for having the singles lead themselves. They will make the plans, instigate them, and have ownership in the ministry. They will be emotionally involved in the ministry, more so than any other type of leadership.

V

SPECIAL FORMS

POSSIBLE CANDIDATES FOR OFFICERS

President:
(1) _____
(2) _____

Vice-president:
(1) _____
(2) _____

Secretary:
(1) _____
(2) _____

Treasurer:
(1) _____
(2) _____

DIRECTORS

Social:
(1) _____
(2) _____

Party:
(1) _____
(2) _____

Recreation:
(1) _____
(2) _____

Care and Concern:
(1) _____
(2) _____

Music:
(1) _____
(2) _____

Attendance Registrar:
(1) _____
(2) _____

Newcomers:
(1) _____
(2) _____

Education:
(1) _____
(2) _____

Service Involvement:
(1) _____
(2) _____

Publicity:
(1) _____
(2) _____

MEMBERSHIP SHEET
Date Joined _____

Name _____ Male _____ Female _____
Address_____
City _____ State _____ Zip _____
Telephone (Home) _____ (Business) _____
Birthday _____/_____/_____
    (Year of birth not necessary)
Number of children _____ Ages of children _____
Names of children _____

Emergency information: In case of emergency and you are
incapacitated who should we call? _____
Phone# _____

Would you be interested in serving on a committee?
Yes _____ No _____

(Please number your #1 choice first, #2 second, and etc)
In what area would you be interested?
Newcomers _____ Party _____ Social _____
Education _____ Care and concern _____
Secretary _____ Attendance _____
Teaching _____
What would you like to teach?

_____

Music _____

(Again, please number them in order of your preference
beginning #1)

In what types of classes would you be the most interested:
Bible study _____ Single living issues _____ Relationship
skills _____

What self-help books would you like to study? _____

_____

_____

Other _____

Would you be interested in participating in a Wednesday night study group? What subjects would you be the most interested in studying?

_____

(Please number them in order of your favorite, beginning with #1)

In what recreational events would you be the most interested?

Camping trips _____ Pizza and movie nights _____
Weekend retreats _____ Volleyball _____ Softball _____
Basketball _____ Bridge _____ Special Saturday night events you would like to attend _____

Please list anything else you would like for the class to start:

_____

_____

How did you hear about our class? _____

_____

General comments about what you have observed about the class:

VISITOR REGISTRATION SHEET

DATE _____

FIRST TIME VISITORS

NAME	ADDRESS	TELEPHONE	
		HOME #	WORK #
1.			
2.			
3.			
4.			
5.			
6.			
7.			
8.			
9.			
10.			
11.			
12.			
13.			
14.			
15.			
16.			
17.			
18.			
19.			
20.			

VISITOR FOLLOW-UPS

NAME OF
CALLER _____ DATE ___ / ___ / ___

DATE	NAME	PHONE #	RESULT
1.			
2.			
3.			
4.			
5.			
6.			
7.			
8.			
9.			
10.			
11.			
12.			
13.			
14.			
15.			
16.			
17.			
18.			
19.			
20.			

CLASS SLAVE AUCTION CONTRACT

CONDITIONS

1. The "SELLER" must sign a contract in advance of the Slave Auction, stating what services they intend to offer to the class.

2. The "BUYER" must pay in cash or by check for services bought on the date of the auction. (A post-dated check not to exceed one week from the date of the auction will be accepted.)

CONTRACT BY THE SELLER

I _____ hereby agree to sell my services for _____, and to the undersigned agree to perform this service within a 60 day period, or on a date agreeable to the buyer, to become effective the date of this sale.

SELLER   X _____ DATE _____

CONTRACT BY THE BUYER

I _____ hereby agree to pay $ _____ for services from the above seller. I also agree to pay in cash payable on the date of the auction, or under the terms stated in the conditions above.

I understand that the monies received from this auction are to be for the benefit of my Sunday school class, _____.

BUYER   X _____ DATE _____

How paid: cash $ _____ check # _____ $ _____

NOMINATION OF CLASS OFFICER

I hereby wish to be nominated for the office of _____ .
I certify that I am a member of _____ church
and the _____ class.

SIGNED _____ DATE _____ / _____ / _____

I wish to nominate _____ for the office of
_____ . I have discussed this with
_____ and they have agreed and know of this
nomination.

SIGNED _____ DATE _____ / _____ / _____

DINNER/BREAKFAST FOR EIGHT SIGN-UP SHEET

DATE OF DINNER/BREAKFAST _____ / _____ / _____

NAME (Please Print)	ADDRESS (Include zip code)	TELEPHONE	
		HOME #	WORK #
1.			
2.			
3.			
4.			
5.			
6.			
7.			
8.			
9.			
10.			
11.			
12.			
13.			
14.			
15.			
16.			
17.			
18.			
19.			
20.			
21.			
22.			
23.			
24.			

25. _____ _____ _____ _____
26. _____ _____ _____ _____
27. _____ _____ _____ _____
28. _____ _____ _____ _____
29. _____ _____ _____ _____
30. _____ _____ _____ _____
31. _____ _____ _____ _____
32. _____ _____ _____ _____
33. _____ _____ _____ _____
34. _____ _____ _____ _____
35. _____ _____ _____ _____
36. _____ _____ _____ _____
37. _____ _____ _____ _____
38. _____ _____ _____ _____
39. _____ _____ _____ _____
40. _____ _____ _____ _____

PLEASE SIGN-UP BELOW IF YOU
CAN BE A HOST/HOSTESS

NAME	ADDRESS	HOME #	WORK #
1. _____	_____	_____	_____
2. _____	_____	_____	_____
3. _____	_____	_____	_____
4. _____	_____	_____	_____
5. _____	_____	_____	_____

(40 guests need 5 hosts/hostesses)

VI

BYLAWS

A set of rules is necessary for any successful organization. As your program begins to grow, bylaws will keep your program organized and structured. This set of bylaws has evolved over the past fifteen years. Everything we have learned about singles ministries is included. Each part is included for a reason. You can modify this set of bylaws to your own group's needs.

Article I. Name:
The name of this church school class is _____
(A brief explanation of the name can be included here.)

Article II. Purposes:
A. To provide a Christian atmosphere where single people may join together in a spirit of friendship and brotherly love.

B. To provide the opportunity for single people to openly discuss their common interests and concerns and to seek Christian understanding.

C. To provide activities in which single people may make new friends and enjoy the company of other singles.

D. To provide support to _____Church.

Article III. Membership:
A. Membership in_____is open to all adult singles whether divorced, widowed, or never married. To become a member, a person shall simply come to _____
(name of your class) at _____ Church (name of

your church). That person will be considered a guest and wear a yellow name tag for the first visit. On the second visit, he or she will wear a pink name-tag, and on the third visit a blue name-tag at which time he or she is considered a new member. On the fourth visit, that person will be considered a full member and will then wear an orange name tag to signify membership in the _____ Class.

Article IV. Board of Directors—The provisions relating to the Board of Directors are as follows:

A. The Board of Directors shall consist of the seventeen elected officers of _____. Each Board member must also be a member of _____ (name of your church). The offices of the class are President, Vice-president, Secretary, Treasurer, Newcomer Director, Attendance Registrar, Care and Concern, Education Director, Music Director, Party Director, Publicity Director, Recreation Director, Service Involvement Director, Technical Director, Single Parenting Director, Social Director, and TLC Director (tender loving care). The senior pastor of the Church and any staff member assigned by the pastor to the singles ministry shall be ex-officio members of the board.

B. Assistants—Each officer, excluding the President and Vice-president, will select an assistant, and one or more committee members, as the officer deems necessary. The assistants must be members of the Church.

C. Term of Office—Ratification—Term of office shall be six months, with new officers assuming official duties on the first Sunday in April or October. Prior to installation in office, the officers and board members are subject to ratification by the Church's Administrative Board.

D. Marriage—If any officer or assistant marries during his/her term of office, he/she will resign immediately from the class and the board of directors.

E. Vacancy of Office—If an officer resigns for any reason during his or her term of office, that office shall be filled by appointment by the Board with consideration being given to the assistant for that office. The Vice-president will fill the office of President, if vacated.

F. Meetings—The Board will have one regular board meeting each month. Special Board meetings may be called anytime by the President when he/she deems it necessary. Board Meetings will be open to any member of _____ (name of your class.)

G. Replacement of Officers—Each office must be represented at Board meetings. If the officer and assistant miss two consecutive meetings with no valid excuse, the remainder of the Board may, by a majority vote, declare that office vacant. The Board will then notify the officer and the assistant, and appoint replacements to fill the vacated office.

H. Vote—Each office shall have one vote at Board meetings.

Article V. Election Procedures:

A. Nominating Committee—The President and the Vice-president shall work together to choose a five member nominating committee. The committee shall be in charge of the elections to be held for the next term. There shall be five persons on the committee consisting of two men and three women, or the reverse. Two of the members shall be officers of the current board. The remaining three members shall be regular members of the class. The committee shall elect its own chairperson. Membership on the committee does not exclude that member from being a candidate for office. Committee members shall wear special badges that designate them as members of the Nominating Committee. The Committee shall determine that each nominated person is qualified to be a candidate for office before that person is nominated. A candidate must have been a member of the church at least sixty days before being nominated. A candidate must attend church services at _____ (name of your church) at least five out of the thirteen Sundays prior to the day of being nominated.

B. Nominating Forms—The Nominating Committee will be in complete charge of providing nominating forms for the class and for collecting those forms. A representative from the committee shall be at the table with the forms on the sixth and seventh Sundays prior to installation of officers.

124

C. Ballot—Taking all nominations in consideration, the committee will choose a ballot of officers to present to the class the fourth and fifth Sundays before installation of officers. The ballot shall consist of at least two nominees for each office if two people willing to fulfill the duties of each office can be found. Candidates shall be listed alphabetically. More than two nominees may be presented. Any person receiving 10 nominating forms turned in with their name will automatically be on the ballot providing he/she is willing to run. All presidential candidates must have prior board experience as either a Board member or assistant for one term from the beginning of the term and attended at least four Board meetings in that position prior to nomination for President. The President and the Vice-president may be listed as a team and not on an individual basis.

D. President—In order to be eligible to be a candidate for President, that person must have been an officer or a member of the board for at least one full term within the previous two years or presently serving as an officer. The candidate must have attended at least two-thirds of the Board meetings, both regular and special. The candidate must attend the class and activities on a regular basis.

E. Candidate Statement—If for any reason a candidate cannot be at the class meeting for his/her candidate speech, a member of the Nominating Committee may read a statement written by the candidate. The Committee member shall state that he/she is not for or against the candidate but simply is reading the speech. The candidate may have a taped message played by a recorder or a video cassette recorder. Each statement is limited to two minutes. Each candidate must run as a separate individual and not with another candidate, other than the President and Vice-president.

F. Absentee Ballot—A member may vote by absentee ballot. The member's name submitting an absentee ballot shall be listed by the Nominating Committee. The casting of the ballot must be witnessed by two members of the Committee. Absentee ballots must be submitted within one week prior to the election.

G. Election Sunday—Election Sunday shall consist of a

general assembly and open fellowship. Class may be held as usual if time permits, and the class so desires. The Nominating Committee shall be in charge of distributing, collecting, and counting the ballots. The chairperson of the Committee shall then present the results of the election to the class.

H. Election—Each officer shall be elected on the basis of a plurality of votes cast for that office. In the event of a tie, successive ballots shall be conducted between the tying candidates until one candidate receives a majority vote.

I. Results—The election results shall be posted in a public place. Candidates may be told of the tally if they so desire. They will be told only of the results of the office for which they ran.

J. Election Celebration—The election celebration for new officers shall be held on the Saturday night just prior to installation Sunday.

K. Time Frame for Election Procedures—Time-frame for election procedures just prior to installation Sunday is as follows:

8th Sunday................ Nominating Committee presented to the class

6th & 7th Sundays...... A representative of the Nominating Committee will have nominating forms available for the class.

4th & 5th Sundays...... Candidates introduced to the class.

3rd Sunday................ Election

2nd Sunday............... Joint Board meeting of old and new officers.

1st Sunday................. Officers serve jointly

Saturday night........... Election Celebration/Dinners for Eight

Installation Sunday..... New officers begin term

Article VI. Duties of Officers

A. President—The President is in charge of the overall planning and motivation of the class. He/she will serve as general spokesperson for the class, will plan and conduct the Sunday morning general assembly, will plan and conduct monthly Board meetings, will establish any special committees or task groups needed, will work closely with church minister to coordinate class activities with the church calendar. The President is a member of the church's Administrative Board and of the Council on Ministries.

B. Vice-president—The Vice-president will plan and organize special events such as fundraising projects, spiritual retreats (reservations will be made one year in advance if possible), will work closely with President and all officers, and will organize and maintain minutes of the class bulletin board. In the absence of the President, he/she shall assume the responsibilities of the President.

C. Secretary—The Secretary will prepare and publish a weekly class bulletin and a monthly calendar of events, take and maintain minutes of the Board meetings, obtain necessary class supplies, and assist the Attendance Registrar in updating and publishing the class directory.

D. Treasurer—The Treasurer will count attendance and collect the offering each Sunday. He/she will count the class offering, giving half to the Church and depositing the other half in the class bank account. Checks made payable to the Church are not included in the class offering, but go directly to the Church. The Treasurer shall maintain a record of receipts and payments and present a written report at the monthly board meetings. He/she will maintain a current record of all class-owned properties, such as typewriters, computers, adding machines, etc. He/she should attend meetings of the Church's Board on Finance and Stewardship.

E. Newcomer Director—The Newcomer Director will organize and coordinate a committee to welcome visitors upon arrival, provide them with a name tag, and introduce them to class members so they will feel welcome and comfortable in the class. He/she will coordinate the Sunday morning Newcomer's classes I and II, which describe the class's goals, purposes, and activities. He/she will conduct a tour of the church for the Newcomer's class II, will plan and conduct a monthly Newcomer's Party to help newcomers feel welcome, maintain Newcomer's Informational packets, maintain and present slide presentations for Newcomer's classes, and be responsible for planning and organizing a weekly Newcomer's gathering. The Newcomer Director will be responsible for sending out invitations to the monthly Newcomer's Party. These should be sent out five days prior to the party. He/she should attend meetings of the Church's Board on Community.

F. Education Director—The Education Director will plan and coordinate weekly Christian education classes and see that the information about these classes is in the bulletin each week, and will work with the Church in reserving rooms for classes. He/she should attend meetings of the Church's Board on Education.

G. Party Director—The Party Director will plan and coordinate all class adult parties, dinners, dances, etc., including handling reservations, deposits, decorations, and supplies. Plans and reservations for the Christmas and New Year's parties should be made one year in advance. He/she should attend meetings of the Church's Board on Community.

H. Social Director—The Social Director will coordinate Dinners for Eight, Saturday Night Live, holiday dinners, and Friday Night Fellowship; and will arrange for coffee on Sunday morning. He/she should attend meetings of the Church's Board on Community.

I. Recreation Director—The Recreation Director will plan and coordinate all class recreational and family-type activities such as picnics, movies, skating parties, zoo trips, museum trips, camping and float trips, etc.; will plan dinner locations after Sunday church services and give such locations to the Secretary to be put in the weekly bulletin and monthly calendars. He/she should attend meetings of the Church's Board on Community.

J. Care and Concern—The Care and Concern Director will organize a committee to contact absent class members, arrange for cards/flowers to be sent in the event of an illness or death of members or their families and notify the church office of such events, organize and maintain a scrapbook and history of the class, organize a committee whose responsibility is to staff the child care provided from 9:00 A.M. to 9:45 A.M. each Sunday, and be responsible for having the Past President's plaque engraved. He/she should attend meetings of the Church's Board on Community.

K. Music Director—The Music Director will plan and organize the music for the Sunday morning class program. He/she will also be responsible for planning and organizing Pickin' 'N' Grinnin'. He/she should attend meetings of the Church's Board on Worship.

L. Attendance Registrar—The attendance registrar will prepare and maintain attendance logs and class roster, make lists of new members for the bulletin, make changes of addresses and new member additions to the directory with assistance of the Secretary, compile and update a class directory three months into the term.

M. Publicity Director—The Publicity Director will be responsible for recording the weekly recorder message with the schedule of events for that week and any necessary updates, and shall be responsible for assisting the other directors in planning and coordinating the publicity of events to the members, and shall be responsible for helping any board members with flyers needed for the class and to see that the class logo is on all flyers to designate approval by the board.

N. Service and Involvement Director—The Service and Involvement Director will organize ways for the class to be involved in providing help and service to the community through existing organizations, directly through the class, or in cooperation with outreach and service activities of the Church. He/she should attend meetings of the Church's Board on Service.

O. Technical Director—The Technical Director shall be responsible for setting up and maintaining the sound system for class events, particularly Sunday morning general assembly.

P. Single Parenting Director—The Single Parenting Director will be responsible for forming a Single Parenting Committee to plan activities for the single parent families of the Church, to reserve all rooms and equipment for such activities, keep a current mailing list for single parents, inform the Church of Single Parenting Committee activities, and see that they are properly advertised in the class and church bulletins. Either the Single Parenting Director or a committee member should attend meetings of the following church boards: Children, Youth, and Single Living.

Q. TLC Director—The TLC director shall attend the Newcomer's class and organize each class into a care group which meets one night per week for the next two consecutive weeks. The TLC Director is responsible for finding two leaders, one male and one female, to be responsible for these follow-up fellowship meetings. The TLC Director should attend meetings of the Church's Board on Community.

R. Activities—All officers should attend class functions and activities regularly and assist where needed in organization.

S. Loyalty—All officers will strive to promote the philosophy of_____(name of your class) as stated in the ideals, goals, and actions set forth in the attached document.

T. Leaving Office—All officers, upon resignation and/or termination of office, shall provide his/her successor with all records, contracts, notes, etc. regarding action taken during the previous term in order to facilitate the next term of officers.

Article VII. General Provisions—General provisions are as follows:

A. Expenses—Any expense, other than normal operating expense, shall be approved by a majority of the Board members present and voted on prior to incurring such expense. Any non-operating expense over $500 shall be brought to the general membership for approval by a majority of those present and voting. Capital expenditures are items that involve equipment. Normal expenses for party costs will not be brought before the membership.

B. Checks—All checks must be cosigned by at least two of the following: President, Vice-president, Secretary, Treasurer, assistant Treasurer, or another designated Board Member.

C. Majority Approval—Bylaws may be amended by the vote of a majority of the Board members present and voting. A quorum of two-thirds of the offices must be represented to take any action requiring a vote.

D. Sponsored Activities—Class-sponsored activities are those activities planned and approved by the Board. Social and recreational activities such as cruises, trips, ski trips, etc., which are not sponsored by the class, may be announced by the members, with prior Board approval, during Sunday morning general assembly. Any distribution of printed material or promotion or advertisement of activities that are not sponsored by the class is prohibited. It is the intent that Class-sponsored activities which are scheduled by the officer in charge be financially self-supporting, specifically including in this sense, social functions such as parties and retreats. Excluded from this provision of self-support are ministry functions such as Holiday Dinners, Newcomer's Parties, Halloween Carnival for all church children, and the Christmas Party for class children.

Article VIII. Amendments:

A. Board Initiated—These bylaws may be amended by a majority vote of the Board of Directors present and voting.

B. Membership Initiated—Bylaw changes may be initiated by the general membership of the class by submitting a referendum petition containing the signatures of 10 percent of the active membership as determined by the Registrar. Written notice of the proposed amendment or change to the bylaws shall be published to the general membership on two consecutive Sundays. The 3rd Sunday the proposed amendment or change will be presented to the general membership and must be approved by a majority of those present and voting.

G. Effective Date of Bylaw Changes—All changes in the bylaws shall apply to the new term of office for the next elected board.

H. Past President's Board—A President's Board shall be formed and shall consist of past presidents of the class. Their function will be an advisory board to the current president. They shall meet as deemed necessary.

The _____ Class

The _____ *Class is* a singles "Family" from diverse backgrounds, with genuine care and concern for one another in the Christian life-style. We believe God wants us to enjoy life, to prosper and be happy in God's service.

We are composed of singles who never married, have divorced, or been widowed from age 20 and up. A wonderful mixture who think young, optimistically, and actively seek life's opportunities.

We offer a caring atmosphere for voluntary participation, without demands, in the class program, one which promotes individual expression and growth in the Spirit of Christ. Participation in all class activities is entirely voluntary, based on your own personal needs not the expectations of others.

Ideals	Goals	Actions
Shares God's Love	Actively worship our living God and endeavor to pass on God's unlimited love.	Demonstrating care and concern for one another in Christian love. Living the Christian life-style, forgiving as we are forgiven
Offers Acceptance	Energetically promote a sense of community within the "Family", all persons are accepted as beautiful.	Accepting everyone regardless of characteristics or personality. Assuming personal responsibility for honesty—"no Games."

132

Supports the Church	Continue to be a valued member of (name of your church) serving as an integral part of the church program and working in co-operation with the minister and his staff.	Active participation in the whole church organization. Class members serving on commissions and committees, coordinating with the minister and staff; performing at least two church services per year.
Meets Differing Spiritual Needs	Provide spiritual growth opportunities for persons with diverse backgrounds, that all may respond according to their varied needs.	—varied religious lessons —personal sharing groups —contemporary retreats —spiritual retreats —covenant groups
Helps One Another	Recognize the "real life" human needs of class members and help meet these needs through a carefully planned program designed to provide understanding and reassurance.	—listening to one another —LEO programs —Divorce Adjustment classes —employment recommendations —trading baby sitting —human sexuality seminars —health education
Is Highly Visible	Publicize the opportunities the class offers so that the whole community knows of them.	—weekly newspaper listing in the singles section —weekly visitor classes
Provides Adult Activities	Sponsor activities for singles with or without a date	—Dinners for Eight —parties and/or dances —dinner-out groups —outdoor trips —bridge clubs

133

Provides
Family
Activities

Conduct group activities where members can bring their children for family fun with both father and mother figures.

—picnics
—skating parties
—lake trips
—ice cream socials
—vacation trips

Grows
Together

Recognize one another's God-given talents and encourage personal growth and development of our full potential.

—honest and sincere sharing of ideas for growth and improvement
—help identify latent abilities
—provide reassurance and courage to reinforce the best in one another

BIBLIOGRAPHY OF RESOURCES FOR SINGLE LIVING

BOOKS

Allen, James. *As a Man Thinketh*. New York: Grosset & Dunlap, 1953.

Atkin, Edith and Estell Rubin. *Part Time Father*. New York: Vanguard, 1976.

Atlas, Stephen. *Single Parenting: A Practical Resource Guide*. Englewood Cliffs, N.J.: Prentice-Hall, 1981.

Bach, George and Ronald Deutsch. *Pairing*. New York: Avon, 1971.

———. *Stop! You're Driving Me Crazy*. New York: Berkeley Publications, 1982.

———. *Creative Aggression: The Art of Assertive Living*. New York: Doubleday, 1983.

Bach, George and Peter Wyden. *The Intimate Enemy: How to Fight Fair*. New York: Avon, 1981.

Bach, Richard. *Illusions: The Adventures of a Reluctant Messiah*. New York: Dell, 1979 .

———. *Jonathan Livingston Seagull*. New York: Avon, 1973.

Baer, Jean. *How to Be an Assertive (Not Aggressive) Woman in Life, in Love, and on the Job*. New York: New American Library, 1976 .

Barback, Lonnie. *For Yourself: The Fulfillment of Female Sexuality*. New York: New American Library, 1976.

Beattie, Melody. *Codependent No More*. San Francisco: Harper & Row, 1987.

Beisser, Arnold R. *The Only Gift*. New York: Doubleday, 1991.

Berne, Eric. *Games People Play*. New York: Ballantine, 1978.

―――. *What Do You Say After You Say Hello?* New York: Bantam, 1975.

Berne, Eric and C. Steiner. *Beyond Games and Scripts*. New York: Ballantine, 1978.

Bloomfield, Harold, et al. *How to Survive the Loss of a Love*. New York: Bantam, 1977.

Bloomfield, Harold and Leonard Felder. *Making Peace with Your Parents*. New York: Random House, 1983.

Bolles, Richard. *What Color Is Your Parachute: A Practical Manual for Job Hunters*. 2nd rev. ed., Berkeley, Calif. Ten Speed Press, 1984.

Bridges, Jerry. *Trusting God—Even When Life Hurts*. Colorado Springs: Navpress, 1988.

Bristow, John T. *What Paul Really Said About Women*. San Francisco: Harper & Row, 1988.

Brothers, Joyce. *What Every Woman Should Know About Men*. New York: Ballantine Books, 1981.

Brown, Helen Gurley. *Sex and the Single Girl*. New York: Avon, 1983.

Buscaglia, Leo. *Love*. New York: Fawcett, 1972.

―――. *Loving Each Other*. New York: Harper & Row, 1984.

―――. *Personhood*. New York: Fawcett, 1978.

―――. *The Way of the Bull*. New York: Fawcett, 1983.

―――. *Living, Loving, and Learning*. New York: Ballantine Books, 1982.

Caine, Les, et al. *Why Be Lonely? A Guide to Meaningful Relationships*. Grand Rapids: Baker Books, 1982.

Cassidy, Robert. *What Every Man Should Know About Divorce*. New York: New Republic Books, 1977 (now out of print).

Colman, Emily and Betty Edwards. *Brief Encounters*. New York: Doubleday, 1979.

Conway, Jim and Sally. *Women in Mid-Life Crisis*. Wheaton, Ill.: Tyndale, 1983.

Coudert, Jo. *The I Never Cooked Before Cookbook*. New York: New American Library, 1972.

Cowan, Connell and Melvyn Kinder. *Smart Women, Foolish Choices*. New York: Crown, 1985.

Crook, Robert. *An Open Book to the Christian Divorce*. Nashville: Broadman Press, 1974 (now out of print).

Dalbey, Gordon. *Healing the Masculine Soul*. Waco, Tex: Word, 1988.

Despert, Louise. *Children of Divorce*. New York: Doubleday, 1953.

Dobson, James C. *Straight Talk to Men*. Waco, Tex: Word, 1984.

Dow, Robert. *Ministry with Single Adults*. Valley Forge: Judson Press, 1977.

Dowling, Colette. *The Cinderella Complex: Women's Hidden Fear of Independence*. New York: Pocket Books, 1982.

Dreikurs, Rudolph and Loren Grey. *Logical Consequences: A New Approach to Discipline*. New York: Dutton, 1968.

Dyer, Wayne. *Gifts From Eykis*. (fiction) New York: Simon and Schuster, 1983.

———. *Your Erroneous Zones*. New York: Simon and Schuster, 1980.

Evans, Michele. *Fearless Cooking for One*. New York: Pocket Books, 1983.

Fagerstrom, Douglas L. *Single to Single*. Wheaton, Ill.: Victor Books, 1991.

Fast, Julius. *Body Language*. New York: Pocket Books, 1984.

Fisher, Bruce. *Rebuilding When Your Relationship Ends*. San Luis Obispo, Calif.: Impact Publishers, 1981.

Forden, Athearn. *How to Divorce Your Wife: The Man's Side of Divorce*. New York: Dorchester Publications, 1977.

Fosdick, Harry E. *The Meaning of Prayer*. Nashville: Abingdon, 1962.

Friedman, Sonya. *Men Are Just Desserts*. New York: Warner Books, 1983.

Fromm, Erich. *The Art of Loving*. New York: Harper and Bros., 1956.

Gardner, Richard. *The Boys And Girls Book About Step-Families*. New York: Bantam, 1985.

Gibran, Kahlil. *The Prophet*. New York: Knopf, 1923.

Gilbert, Sara. *How to Live with a Single Parent*. New York: Lothrop, Lee, & Shepard Books, 1982.

Girdano, Daniel and George Everly. *Controlling Stress and Tension: A Holistic Approach*. Englewood Cliffs, N.J.: Prentice-Hall, 1979.

Givens, David. *Love Signals: How to Attract a Mate*. New York: Crown, 1983.

Goldberg, Herb. *Hazards of Being Male*. New York: New American Library, 1977.

———. *New Male*. New York: New American Library, 1980.

———. *The New Male-Female Relationship*. New York: Signet, 1984.

Goldstine, Daniel, et al. *The Dance-Away Lover*. New York: Ballantine, 1978.

Gordon, Thomas. *Parent Effectiveness Training*. New York: New American Library, 1975.

Gore, Tipper. *Raising PG Kids in an X-Rated Society*. Nashville: Abingdon, 1987.

Greenwald, Harold and Elizabeth Rich. *The Happy Person*. Briarcliff Manor, N.Y.: Stein and Day, 1984.

Greenwald, Jerry. *Be the Person You Were Meant to Be*. New York: Dell, 1979.

Halpern, Howard. *How to Break Your Addiction to a Person*. New York: Bantam, 1982.

Harragan, Betty. *Games Mother Never Taught You*. New York: Warner, 1982.

Harris, Thomas. *I'm OK—You're OK*. New York: Avon, 1982.

Harvey, Joan C. and Cynthia Katz. *If I'm So Successful, Why Do I Feel LIke a Fake?* New York: St. Martin's, 1985.

Hendrix, Harville. *Getting the Love You Want*. New York: Harper & Row, 1988.

Hyatt, Ralph. *Before You Love Again*. New York: McGraw-Hill, 1980.

———. *Before You Marry Again*. New York: Random House, 1977 (out of print).

Hyde, Margaret O. *My Friend Has Four Parents*. New York: McGraw-Hill, 1981.

James, Muriel and Louis Savarz. *The Heart of Friendship*. New York: Harper & Row, 1978.

Johnson, Stephen. *First Person Singular: Living the Good Life Alone*. New York: New American Library, 1978.

Jongeward, Dorothy and Dru Scott. *Women As Winners: Transactional Analysis for Personal Growth*. Reading, Mass.: Addison-Wesley, 1976.

Kesler, Jay. *Ten Mistakes Parents Make with Teenagers (And How to Avoid Them)*. Brentwood, Tenn.: Wolgemuth & Hyatt, 1988.

Klein, Carole. *Single Parent Experience*. New York: Avon, 1978.

Kopp, Sheldon. *An End to Innocence: Facing Life Without Illusions*. New York: Bantam, 1981.

Krantzler, Mel. *Creative Divorce*. New York: New American Library, 1975.

———. *Learning to Love Again*. New York: Bantam, 1979.

Kübler-Ross, Elisabeth. *Questions on Death and Dying*. New York: MacMillan, 1974.

Kushner, Harold. *When Bad Things Happen to Good People*. New York: Avon, 1983.

———. *When All You've Ever Wanted Isn't Enough*. New York: Summit Books, 1985.

———. *Who Needs God*. New York: Pocket Books, 1989.

Laborde, Genie Z. *Influencing With Integrity*. Palo Alto, Calif.: Syntony Publishing, 1983.

———. *Fine Tune Your Brain*. Pala Alto, Calif.: Syntony, 1988.

Lair, Jess. *I Ain't Much Baby—But I'm All I've Got*. New York: Fawcett, 1972.

Lasswell, Marcia and Norma Lobsenz. *Styles of Loving: Why You Love the Way You Do*. New York: Ballantine, 1981.

Lenz, Elinor and Marjorie Shaevitz. *So You Want to Go Back to School*. New York: McGraw-Hill, 1977 (out of print).

Lyon, Harold. *Tenderness Is Strength: From Machismo to Manhood*. New York: Harper & Row, 1977 (out of print).

Mace, David. *The Christian Response to the Sexual Revolution*. Nashville: Abingdon, 1970.

McGinnis, Alan Loy. *The Friendship Factor*. Minneapolis: Augsburg, 1979.

McGinnis, Alan Loy. *The Romance Factor*. New York: Harper & Row, 1982.

————. *How to Succeed at Being Yourself*. Minneapolis, Augsburg, 1987.

Mains, David and Karen. *In His Steps*. Waco, Tex.: Word, 1988.

Mandino, Og. *A Better Way to Live*. New York: Bantam, 1990.

————. *The Choice*. New York: Bantam, 1984.

————. *The Christ Commission*. New York: Bantam, 1981.

————. *The Greatest Miracle in the World*. New York: Bantam, 1977.

————. *The Greatest Salesman in the World*. New York: Bantam, 1974.

————. *Og Mandino's University of Success*. New York: Bantam, 1982.

————. *Mission: Success!* New York: Bantam, 1986.

Marshall, Catherine. *Beyond Ourselves*. Tappan, N.J.: Chosen Books, 1984.

Martin, John R. *Divorce and Remarriage*. Scottsdale, Penn.: Herald Press, 1974.

Martin, Norma and Zola Levitt. *Divorce: A Christian Dilemma*. Scottsdale, Penn.: Herald Press, 1977.

Maslow, Abraham. *The Farther Reaches of Human Nature*. New York: Viking, 1971.

Mayer, Nancy. *The Male Mid-Life Crisis: Fresh Starts After 40*. New York: New American Library, 1970.

Miller, Alice. *Prisoners of Childhood*. New York: Basic Books, 1981.

Miller, Keith. *Habitation of Dragons*. Waco, Tex.: Word, 1981.

————. *A Hunger for Healing*. San Francisco: HarperCollins, 1991.

————. *The Taste of a New Wine*. Waco, Tex.: Word, 1967.

Miller, Keith and Andrea. *The Single Experience*. Waco, Tex.: Word, 1981.

Minirth, Frank, Paul Meier, and Don Hawkins. *Worry-Free Living*. Nashville: Thomas Nelson, 1989.

Monat, Alan, and Richard S. Lazarus, eds. *Stress and Coping*. New York: Columbia University Press, 1985.

Moore, James M. *Yes, Lord, I Have Sinned, But I Have Several Excellent Excuses*. Nashville: Abingdon, 1991.

Naisbitt, John. *Megatrends: Ten New Directions Transforming Our Lives.* New York: Warner Books, 1983.

Neumann, Mildred and Bernard Berkowitz. *How to Be Your Own Best Friend.* New York: Ballantine, 1981.

Nir, Yehuda and Bonnie Maslin. *Loving Men for All the Right Reasons.* New York: Dell, 1983.

Noble, June and William. *How to Live With Other People's Children.* New York: E. P. Dutton, 1979.

Paulus, Trina. *Hope for the Flowers.* Mahwah, N.J.: Paulist Press, 1972.

Peale, Norman Vincent. *Positive Imaging: The Powerful Way to Change Your Life.* New York: Revell, 1981.

Peck, M. Scott. *People of the Lie.* New York: Simon and Schuster, 1983.

―――. *The Road Less Traveled.* New York: Simon and Schuster, 1980.

Peters, Thomas and Robert Waterman. *In Search of Excellence.* New York: Warner Books, 1984.

Powell, John. *The Secret of Staying in Love.* Allen, Tex.: Argus, 1974.

―――. *Unconditional Love.* Allen, Tex.: Tabor, 1978.

―――. *Why Am I Afraid to Tell You Who I Am?* Allen, Tex.: Argus, 1969.

Raphael, Beverly. *The Anatomy of Bereavement.* New York: Basic Books, 1983.

Reed, Bobbie. *I Didn't Plan to Be a Single Parent!* St. Louis: Concordia, 1981.

Rubin, Theodore. *The Angry Book.* New York: MacMillan, 1970.

―――. *Compassion and Self-Hate.* New York: Ballantine, 1976.

―――. *One to One.* Pinnacle Books, 1984.

Russianoff, Peniople. *Why Do I Think I Am Nothing Without a Man?* New York: Bantam, 1982.

Schwambach, Stephen and Judith. *For Lovers Only.* Eugene, Oreg.: Harvest House, 1990.

Seaburg, David. *The Art of Selfishness.* New York: Pocket Books, 1981.

Shain, Merle. *When Lovers Are Friends.* New York: Bantam, 1980.

Shain, Merle. *Some Men Are More Perfect Than Others.* New York: Bantam, 1980.

Sheehy, Gail. *Pathfinders.* New York: William Morrow & Co., 1981.

———. *Passages.* New York: Bantam, 1977.

Siegelman, Ellen Y. *Personal Risk: Mastering Change in Love and Work.* New York: Harper & Row, 1983.

Simundson, Daniel J. *Faith Under Fire.* San Francisco: HarperCollins, 1991.

Smith, Manuel. *When I Say No, I Feel Guilty.* New York: Bantam, 1974.

Smith, Harold I. *Forty Something, and Single.* Wheaton, Ill.: Victor Books, 1991.

Smoke, Jim. *Growing Through Divorce.* Eugene, Oreg.: Harvest House, 1984.

———. *Living Beyond Divorce.* Eugene, Oreg.: Harvest House, 1976.

———. *Suddenly Single.* Old Tappan, N.J.: Revell, 1984.

Sroka, Barbara. *One Is a Whole Number.* Wheaton, Ill.: Victor Books, 1978.

Stearns, Ann K. *Living Through Personal Crisis.* New York: Ballantine Books, 1984.

Steiner, Claude. *Scripts People Live.* New York: Bantam, 1975.

Stone, Hal, and Sidra Windelman. *Embracing Ourselves.* Marina del Rey, Calif.: DeVorss and Co., 1985.

Swindoll, Charles R. *Strengthening Your Grip.* Waco, Tex.: Word, 1982.

Viorst, Judith. *Necessary Losses.* New York: Simon and Schuster, 1986.

Viscott, David. *The Language of Feelings.* New York: Pocket Books, 1977.

———. *Risking.* New York: Pocket Books, 1979.

Wagner, Maurice E. *The Sensation of Being Somebody.* New York: Harper & Row, 1975.

Waitley, Dennis E. *Seeds of Greatness.* Old Tappan, N.J.: Revell, 1983.

Wanderer, Zev and Tracy Cabot. *Letting Go: A 12-Week Personal Action Program to Overcome a Broken Heart.* New York: Warner Books, 1979.

BIBLIOGRAPHY

Weatherhead, Leslie. *Christian Agnostic*. Nashville: Abingdon, 1979.

Weisinger, Hendrie, and Norman M. Lobsenz. *Dr. Weisinger's Work-Out Book*. New York: Quill, 1985.

Williams, Robert A. *Journey Through Life*. Nashville: Thomas Nelson Publishers, 1991.

Woititz, Janet G. *Struggle for Intimacy*. Deerfield Beach, Fla.: 1985.

Wright, H. Norman. *How to Get Along With Almost Anyone*. Waco, Tex.: Word, 1989.

Yankelovich, Daniel. *New Rules: Searching for Self-Fulfillment in a World Turned Upside Down*. New York: Random House, 1981.

Zilbergeld, Bernie. *Male Sexuality*. New York: Bantam, 1978.

MAGAZINES

Cosmopolitan
S Magazine
Single!
New Woman
Self
SOLO